Fake, Fact, and Fantasy
Children's Interpretations
of Television Reality

LEA's COMMUNICATION SERIES
Jennings Bryant/Dolf Zillmann, General Editors

Titles in Media Education (Robert Kubey/Renee Hobbs, Advisory Editors) include:

Davies * Fake, Fact, and Fantasy: Children's Interpretations of Television Reality

Fake, Fact, and Fantasy
Children's Interpretations
of Television Reality

Máire Messenger Davies

LEA LAWRENCE ERLBAUM ASSOCIATES, PUBLISHERS
1997 Mahwah, New Jersey

Lawrence Erlbaum Associates, Inc., Publishers
10 Industrial Avenue
Mahwah, New Jersey 07430

Cover design by Kathryn Houghtaling

Library of Congress Cataloging-in-Publication Data

Davies, Máire Messenger.
    Fake, fact, and fantasy : children's interpreta-
tions of television reality / by Máire Messenger
Davies.
        p. cm.
    Includes bibliographical references and index.
    ISBN 0-8058-2046-9 (alk. paper). — ISBN 0-
8058-2047-7 (pbk. : alk. paper)
        1. Television and children—United States. 2. Social
perception in children—United States. 3. Cognition in
children—United States. 4. Visual literacy—United
States. I. Title.
    HQ784.T4D38   1996
    302.23'45'083—dc21   96–9530
                                                  CIP

Books published by Lawrence Erlbaum Associates are
printed on acid-free paper, and their bindings are
chosen for strength and durability.

Printed in the United States of America
10 9 8 7 6 5 4 3 2 1

Contents

Dedicated to the memory of my father, Terry Messenger

My first storyteller

1916–1995

Preface

This book is based on research carried out at the Annenberg School for Communication, University of Pennsylvania, in 1993. I was privileged to be one of the first group of Annenberg Research Fellows, a group of visiting scholars supported by the school in carrying out research on a particular topic. Our topic that first year was Media Literacy in Children, and my four fellow scholars (Roger Desmond, Dafna Lemish, Robert Kubey, and Tamar Liebes), myself, and the head of the Fellowship Program, Elihu Katz, debated long and energetically about what this term might mean.

Some of the results of these deliberations are in this book, and I apologize to my distinguished colleagues if I have not done justice to their ideas and expertise in my treatment of our subject. I am aware that there are other, fuller, or more precise definitions of the term *media literacy* than the ones I write about here—but this is how it turned out for me. I am extremely grateful to the Annenberg School for the opportunity of carrying out the project, and I would like to express my thanks not only for its financial support, but also to its teaching, library, computing, and office staff for their help and kindness. I would particularly like to thank the graduate students who helped with the data collection and analysis in this project: Andrea McDonald, Darin Klein, and Bill Mikulak.

The other group of people without whom the project could not have been completed are the children who are the subjects of the book. Enormous thanks are due to the boys and girls of Chestnut Hill Academy and Springside School, Philadelphia, for sharing their ideas and insights so freely and eloquently.[1] Again, I am conscious of not doing full justice to the insights, imagination, and intelligence of my young subjects; they gave me far more than could be dealt with in full here. It was a great privilege to talk to them, and I wish them success in the rest of their school careers. Thanks are also due to the principals of the schools, to the parents, and to the children's class teachers for their sympathetic cooperation in setting up the project.

Finally, I would like to pay tribute to my former colleagues and students in the College of Communication, Boston University, where I was working

---

[1]The children's names have been changed.

as Associate Professor of Broadcasting at the time of the Fellowship—and not just for giving me time off. I learned to respect the art and craft of television production from my friends at BU. Although I am now back in my native city of London (working here, too, alongside skilled media professionals at the London College of Printing's School of Media), I hope that my American influences will stay with me. Surprising though it may seem to some colleagues in the United States, many of us teachers and students on this side of the Atlantic believe that American culture has greatly enriched our own. The American courtesy and hospitality we encountered is gratefully remembered by all the family.

Thanks to Steve Cameron in Boston for advice on computing, and to Godfrey Lee at the LCPDT, for the same, and to Huw Davies for backup help.

Finally, as always, thanks to my family—John, Tom, Hannah, Huw, and Eli—for being tolerant of the hours spent with the powerbook, for their useful ideas and criticisms, and for taking my mind off it when necessary.

—*Máire Messenger Davies*

1

The Mediated World: The Uses of Media Literacy

"Is that a real train?"

(Small boy, aged about three, to his mother, as they stood on
a suburban station platform, watching the London train approach.)

What idea of a train was in this little boy's mind when he asked this
question? The question implied that the little boy had some conception
of "unreal" trains against which he was comparing this one. Would this
conception of real/unreal be based on experience of pictures? Or stories?
Or fantasy play? Or television, or film, or toys, all of which, as an urban
child in the 1990s, he would have had experience of? Perhaps this little
boy was comparing the oncoming train to a toy train; or he might have
been thinking of a televised train like Thomas the Tank Engine. Both have
elements of reality and unreality; for instance, you can play with one, but
not with the other. On the other hand, Thomas the Tank Engine, although
it only appears in the flat, pictorial world of television, moves by itself
and has properly scaled human figures walking round it. The train in the
distance obviously raised some of these questions in this toddler's mind.

VISUAL LITERACY

Perhaps the oncoming London train presented a perceptual problem of
perspective to the little boy. Perhaps, in the distance, it looked as small as
a toy, or as flat as a picture to him. It did not to me, but then, I do not
consciously notice things like perspective any more. I long ago internal-
ized the habit of using depth and distance cues to assess the size and
proximity of objects, probably when I was a baby. Recognizing the
artificial techniques of representing distance in a picture is different,

1

though. I distinctly remember the first time I noticed the artistic technique of perspective. I was six years old and there was a poster on the wall of my school classroom with a representation of a path converging to a point on the horizon. I realized that if I wanted to make *my* drawings of paths look "real," I had to draw converging lines, like an upturned V, instead of parallel ones. I was very proud of my discovery and all my own drawings from then on had upturned-V paths in them. Later I realized that a lot of other people had already made this discovery, and even later, to my surprise, I found out that artistic perspective was not just something to be stumbled upon; it was also the product of an early form of artistic technology; artists like Leonardo had used special gadgets to view distant scenes and to mathematically represent the relationship between objects in space on the canvas.

This raises the question of whether we understand the artistic techniques by which real-life distance and dimensions are artificially represented through inborn instinct, or whether this knowledge has to be acquired through cultural experience and education. As in my case, it is probably a little of both. But artistic perspective does seem to be unique to certain kinds of culture and not to others, as Paul Messaris' 1994 book, *Visual Literacy*, discussed. Messaris did not believe that this is because different cultures have fundamentally different ways of seeing things. He argued that the perceptual processes we use in working out the shape, nearness, and relationship of objects in the real world are the same abilities that we use in interpreting pictures. Hence, he proposed, even people unfamiliar with perspective ought to be able to make sense of it, just as people who have grown up in totally flat landscapes can still work out what a mountain or a tall building is.

This raises the further question of whether people have to be taught to be visually literate. Despite the fact that we use our eyes quite efficiently to interpret visual information every moment of our waking lives, the term *visual literacy* implies that there are some visual techniques we cannot master without help.

The use of the term *literacy* when applied to print is comparatively uncontentious. Reading and writing are rare skills, which most of us cannot acquire on our own. To acquire them, we need access to written materials, and we have to be taught how to make sense of these materials. The printed word, as Messaris pointed out, has only an arbitrary relationship to meaning. Hence it is difficult for an untaught person to work out the relationship between the abstract markings on a page and spoken language (which, of course, is arbitrary too, in that there is no intrinsic relationship between sound and sense). The comparative rarity and specialization of print literacy has made it culturally valuable; literacy means power. Spoken language, on the other hand, can be mastered by anybody by the time they are four or so, no matter how low-class or uncivilized they are. This very much reduces the cultural value of oral traditions; if any ignorant peasant can do it, it cannot be very special, can it? And visual literacy? Or media literacy? What is special about them? Why, and how, should we have to be taught to make sense of pictures or, even more vaguely, of media? *Media* could mean anything from huge broadcasting institutions and the way they are run and financed, to the use of your fingers to write messages in the sand. How does anyone become media-literate? Do we pick up our knowledge of modern audiovisual media automatically from exposure to them, or does acquiring this knowledge require rare and special skills, like reading print, which we have to be taught?

NATURE AND NURTURE

The nature/nurture argument, of which the debate about whether children have to be taught to 'read' television is a recent offshoot, has long-standing political implications; human abilities that seem to be natural are often undervalued, whereas skills that are laboriously acquired by small groups of people, end up labeled as "elite," and can earn great rewards. Clearly, any type of information that can attach the title "literacy" to itself, can make claims for being special—for being included in the school curriculum, for instance, and acquiring budgets and personnel. The politics of the argument can obscure the commonsense fact that, for young children, it is an irrelevant argument. All human skills require *both* natural ability and environmental encouragement in the form of budgets and personnel, and this is particularly evident in the skills of symbolic representation, of which spoken language is an excellent example.

The little boy on the station, in common with 3-year-olds all over the world, was able to speak in sentences. Reaching this stage of linguistic development around the third year of life seems to be universal, which suggests that it is biologically programmed (Lenneberg, 1967). However, the little boy's language was English, his accent was pure Cockney, and his knowledge of real trains probably came from travel, all of which could only be the result of local and specific cultural experiences. Furthermore, his question was addressed to his mother in the confident knowledge that she would hear, understand, and answer; without her, or somebody like her, he could not have reached such a sophisticated stage of linguistic development so young.

Children are born with an innate human capacity to learn. They also need to learn to understand the world in which they live, including the way that it is represented in different symbolic forms. These vary, depending on when and where we live, and each generation of children has to come to terms with these variations. Some of the skills of making sense of symbolic representation can be picked up by children, so long as they have access to such representations. (My "discovery" of perspective is an example.) But literacy in its widest sense requires learned and taught skills. Literacy, in the sense in which it is increasingly used today, is about enabling the developing child to understand and use the many abstract systems underpinning the various representations of the real world with which he or she is surrounded: the printed word; logic; mathematics; scientific models; musical harmony; computer languages; visual displays; artistic structures of various kinds, including the 'realistic' audiovisual narratives of television and film.

All these structures have some relationship with the real world. The connection may be arbitrary, as in the case of written language, where we have to be taught to understand the link between the mysterious grouping of letters in the word C-A-T, as it appears in a young child's picture book, and the furry animal which says "miaow." Or the relationship may be more directly representational and iconic, as in the case of the photograph of the cat on the facing page in the book. A baby can identify the picture, but not the word, which suggests that visual literacy comes a lot more easily and naturally than does print literacy. However, even in photographs and realistic paintings, the relationship between a real-world object and its representation is never direct. As the grammatical transformations of speech—negations, tenses, emphases—signal different versions of meaning, so objects, people, and experiences in the real world also go through a series of transformations in the process of being translated into an artistic or media representation. It is these transformations, and children's awareness of them, that are discussed in this book.

The book is concerned particularly with the audiovisual narratives of television and film. It is a fundamental premise of the book—borne out by the research described in it—that the "realism" of film and television genres is only apparent. The naturalistic qualities of soap opera, situation comedy, and children's drama, as well as the "real" people and events in non-fiction programs such as TV news, are the product of a great deal of human artifice, and they operate according to rules and conventions quite as complex as the five-act structure of Jacobean drama or the sculptured representations of history in the friezes on the Parthenon. Unlike these examples, which thanks to the passing of time, we can all recognize as Art, or Culture, to be analyzed and appreciated, the daily conventions of television programs are so familiar, domesticated, and naturalized as to appear more like life than like art. Even adult critics talk about television fiction as if it were really happening; the cartoon characters, the Simpsons, for example, are often described as a dysfunctional family. Nevertheless, even the youngest viewers have some sense of the artifice of television, and older children have much more interesting ideas about the medium than are generally discussed. It was to explore children's awareness of the submerged conventions of television genres, of their functions and per-ceived effects, of their relationship to the real world, and of how this awareness varies with age and other factors, that the study described in this book was carried out.

THE REAL WORLD

For the modern child, brought up from babyhood with apparently realistic representations of recognizable people talking to her from a box in the corner, a knowledge of the rules of different representational systems, whether picked up or taught in media education classes, is only half the story. To be truly literate, the modern child also needs to have a body of knowledge about the real world, against which the various symbolic representations of it can be measured. The relationship between the real and the represented (or mediated) is probably *the* central intellectual question for a late 20th century child, as my 3-year-old friend on the station correctly realized. Any assessment of children's media literacy has to be concerned with their understandings of the relationship between the real and the representational.

MASS PRODUCED CULTURE: A CAUSE FOR PESSIMISM?

The cultural products of the Western world in the last half of this century, and the myriad ways in which the reality of the world is represented or mediated are greater and more accessible for young children now than they have ever been. From the time-honored picture book, now using high-definition photographs, through television, computer games, and virtual reality, visual and audiovisual representations of the world have become more and more sophisticated, more and more like the real thing, and more and more pervasive. Furthermore, as children in industrialized societies lose their freedom to walk the streets and fields, these mediated forms are an increasingly important source of information for them about the outside world.

There are those who view these developments with pessimism. Cultural commentators such as George Gerbner and Neil Postman lament the fact that young human beings no longer receive their cultural products from their own communities, but from mass-produced entertainment, provided for them by huge commercial organizations whose primary concern is profit. There is something sad to those of us who grew up in the (just) pre-TV age, about the thought that children prefer to sing commercial jingles, or the songs from a Disney movie, rather than old nursery rhymes (many of which were adult products, often referring to topics not at all suitable for children—Georgie Porgie for instance.) Stories about children not being allowed to walk to school by themselves, or having to be taught playground games by grown-ups are certainly depressing. There is much adult concern, too, about the realistic violence that children are able to see on television and video. Some people are concerned about this because they believe that children do not know the difference between reality and fantasy on TV, and, therefore, are more likely to be harmed by it. Others argue that children *do* know the difference between TV fantasy and reality, or can be taught about it, and, hence, can be protected against harmful effects. The idea that knowing that something is unreal protects us from harmful effects needs to be critically examined, and this is one of the lines of inquiry described in this book.

I tend to line up with the cultural optimists on these questions, not because I approve of exposing children (even those who know the difference between reality and fantasy) to exotic and realistic media representations of torture: I do not. My optimism comes from my respect for the developing human organism and its huge capacity for adaptive learning. Evolution has programmed human children to be flexible, adaptable, and competent learners, so that they can accommodate themselves to whatever conditions of society in which they happen to find themselves. Such conditions are very various, and they have never been perfect. But given a very few essential requirements—food, shelter, love—and reasonably stable social arrangements in which adults can provide these things, human children will usually grow up into competent adults. Human children as a breed are not pessimistic at all. They want and need to learn, and the world is an interesting place to them because of the opportunities for learning it presents. We adults may be nervous about computers. Six-year-olds are not.

THE CHALLENGE OF MODERN MEDIA

How do children adapt to, and learn from, modern media? What do mediated representations such as television and film mean to them? Children need to work out the relationship between the real world of their own experience and the mediated world they see on TV, in films, in pictures, and increasingly nowadays, on computer screens, and we need to know what strategies they use to do this. It is particularly important for them to have ways of deciding what to *believe* of what they see and hear. Modern media offer a bewildering variety of cues about what is reliable information and what is not. For instance, TV news presenters routinely address the camera, whereas actors in a drama almost never do; facing the camera is, thus, a reality (or, to use a linguistics term that recurs in this book, a *modality*) cue about whether a program is fact or fiction.

Many researchers and teachers are interested in how and when young children learn these cues. Do they learn them by themselves? Or are they duped by the clever techniques of directors and editors into believing things that are not true, or that are not good for them? Does this matter? After all, most traditional culture and art forms—paintings, sculptures, plays, operas, novels, poetry—which we adults tend to think of as good, are designed to deceive us, too. Of course, there are other pleasures and truths that we can gain in the process of yielding to these deceptions, of willingly suspending our disbelief, as the poet Samuel Taylor Coleridge put it. But deceiving children is somehow seen as especially wrong, in a way that is less often applied to adult media and culture; the young, as critics since Plato have been reminding us, are supposed to be told the truth. But is reality the same as truth, and is being seen as real the only criterion for judging something's value? What do children themselves think?

The research described in this book addresses some of these questions by asking children themselves about their reality, or modality, judgments about different kinds of television and exploring their reasons for these judgments. Despite the increasing proliferation of new media like computers and interactive technology, which raise interesting new questions about literacy, I concentrate on television for two reasons: First, it is still the most pervasive and popular form of entertainment and leisure-time activity in the industrialized world, for both children and adults. Second, and more importantly from the perspective of an interest in literacy, television, particularly the kinds of popular drama enjoyed by children, has deep roots in literature. The link between literacy and literature is not only etymological but cultural. The definition of television adopted in this study is not that of a "one-eyed monster" or a "plug-in drug"—to quote some of the wilder adult fantasies about it—but of a body of literature to which children are regularly exposed.

The study is an attempt to explore more deeply some of children's ideas about the medium of television and how it works: its messages; its artifice; its techniques; its aims; its effects; its usefulness to themselves and to other children. These are children's views. They are different from adults' views. I hope that they help to develop some fuller answers to the question posed at the beginning of this chapter. When a child asks whether something is real or not, the first question an adult needs to ask is, What do you mean by real?

2

The Real World —
and the Real Child

Many studies about cultural forms such as television concentrate on the medium itself. The content is analyzed for incidents of violence, or of political bias, or for representations (or misrepresentations) of women and other groups. However, media analysts have begun to acknowledge that the meanings of cultural products are not only fixed by the producers (important though the producers are), but are also negotiated by audiences. Different people will read things differently. Where children are concerned, the readings they produce and the meanings they infer from stories, TV programs, films, and other experiences are constrained, to invoke a term used in developmental psychology, not just by taste, experience, or educational level; they are also constrained by the stage of development that the child has reached.

As every parent knows, children develop and grow at different rates, and with great individual variation; no two children are alike, even twins. However, starting at birth and continuing through to adulthood, every parent also knows that children go through dramatic, inevitable changes in growth, in behavior, and in skills, and many of these changes are common to all children, everywhere, regardless of culture, such as the physical changes brought about by puberty.

In this chapter, some developmental issues—or constraints—relevant to the question of how children understand the representations of the real world (for example, as seen in different kinds of television programming), are discussed, particularly the constraints concerned with symbolic processing. The term *constraint* is used by developmental psychologists, such as Howard Gardner in his book, *The Unschooled Mind* (1991), to define the limitations imposed by age and immaturity on what children can and cannot do. The idea that there are such things as developmental, or

8

biological, constraints on children's behavior and performance is another nature/nurture issue, and as such, can be contentious. For instance, in an essay about young people's media use (Buckingham, 1993b), media-studies lecturer David Buckingham, of the Institute of Education at London University, argued that "childhood is not *merely* [my emphasis] a biological phenomenon . . . it has been constructed in very different ways in different cultures and in different historical periods; . . . age is a social category, not *merely* a biological one"(p.15).

Developmental psychologists accept the importance of environmental influences, but, like developmental pediatricians and others who study childhood professionally with a view to helping children, they would not describe biology as "mere." Inherited biological characteristics such as facial appearance, physique, skin color, sex, predisposition to illnesses of various kinds, likeness or unlikeness to parents—all can profoundly affect the way individuals are able to live their lives. Gardner argues, from empirical research, that strong and consistent differences can also be observed between different age groups in all kinds of ways, and in all kinds of culture. Many of these differences, he argues, are a product of "developmental constraints," arising from the genetically programmed nature of human children.

AGE DIFFERENCES

Age differences are a standard measure of developmental variation. Many human skills (though not all) improve and become more complex as children get older. Some human skills, such as language acquisition, seem to be exercised more competently in younger children than in older people, but more complex expressions of language, such as literary writing, technical reading, or advanced oratory, are obviously exercised more competently by adults than by infants. Age differences were a variable in the study described in this book. This was because, regardless of one's views about their origin, they are useful benchmarks against which to try to understand how a 5-year-old, or an 8-year-old is getting on. If a 5-year-old proves to be as articulate and knowledgeable as an 8-year-old, and an 8-year-old shows more imaginative reasoning than a 10-year-old, this tells us something useful about the potential capacity of 5-year-olds, 8-year-olds, and 10-year-olds: maybe they can cope with more advanced books or lessons than we have been giving them. But we cannot make this discovery without having some general expectations drawn from large numbers of observations of different-aged children.

Hence, from the point of view of parents and teachers who have to deal with children on a day-to-day basis, theoretical arguments about the relative contributions of biology and culture need to be translated into reasonable practical guidelines as to what can and cannot be expected of children as they grow from helpless infancy through the different stages of their childhoods, en route to reproductive maturity (the biological, if not social, definition of adulthood) at around the age of 13 to 16. It can help, for instance, to know that tantrums around the age of two are normal, that many intelligent children do not talk much until they are three, that 8-year-old (but not 18-year-old) girls can run just as fast as boys the same age, that girls start their adolescent growth spurt some time between 10 and 12, on average two years ahead of boys, and so on. This knowledge about what is, on the whole, normal can be reassuring and helpful for parents and teachers, so long as it is not used prescriptively to insist that *all* 2-year-olds, even mild and peaceable ones, must have tantrums and that all 8-year-old girls must be forced to run as fast as their brothers. This would seem almost too banally commonsensical to need saying, if it were not for the fact that many arguments about children and the media ignore developmental processes.

MEMBERSHIP OF THE TRIBE

Knowledge about what can broadly be expected of different aged children can help to defuse some of the controversy surrounding children's use of mass media. Take, for instance, the case of persuasive advertising messages suggesting to children that they need certain kinds of very expensive footwear to be cool. The exposure of children to these kinds of commercial persuasions has been described by a number of writers, such as Neil Postman (1985), as utterly destructive of childhood, because childhood, to Postman, is almost exclusively a cultural and not a biological construct. Now that children are massively exposed to adult cultural products in the form of commercial television, he argues, childhood no longer exists.

However, if we take a proper developmental view of childhood, which recognizes the powerful interaction between biological change and educational input, childhood becomes much less easy to get rid of. The messages provided for children by adults, whether in the home or in the school, or through mass media, can never have an undiluted impact. All education, including the culture outside school, has to work within the constraints of child growth and development. The interaction between heredity and environment is so profound that attempts to modify child behavior without taking the nature of childhood into account are unlikely to work, as Howard Gardner (1991) pointed out in his extended analysis of "the unschooled mind" of the preschool child and its resistance to formal instruction. The example just given, of promoting sneakers through TV ads, illustrates this interaction. The ads exploit the natural tendency of children in middle childhood to congregate in peer groups (particularly same-sex ones) and to have certain kinds of "tribal" rituals and symbols, such as special shoes or clothing, which exclude adults. These kinds of behavior have long historical roots.

In their pioneering work, *The Lore and Language of Schoolchildren* (1959, revised 1986), Iona and Peter Opie described many childhood rituals of partisanship: "chants, songs and slogans" to indicate support for political parties, sports teams, schools, religious groups, and neighborhood gangs. The Opies found that the habit of identifying your group by colors and clothing was expressed in ancient chants such as "Blues blues, always lose" or "Reds, reds, wet their beds" (p. 352). Marketing strategies that exploit the desire to be cool acknowledge this universal childhood "tribalism." Marketing strategies are not, by themselves, causing children to behave in completely new ways. Although selling techniques have become very much more sophisticated thanks to mass media, they only work because they skillfully utilize knowledge about the traditional norms of the behavior of children and young people in groups. If human children did not continue to socialize and identify themselves through group rituals, coolness would not be a selling point. The problem of excessive consumerism among the young is a genuine one for adults, but the problem is as much a product of children's natural desire to be part of a peer group as it is of clever advertising techniques. It is this interaction between nature and nurture that we need to understand if we are to educate the young effectively about modern society and its cultural activities.

LAYERS OF SYMBOLIC SOPHISTICATION

The development of the skills of symbolic processing seems to be programmed to help children make increasingly sophisticated judgments about the relationship between the real world and symbolic representations of it. In *The Unschooled Mind*, Howard Gardner (1991) described the sorts of reasoning that seem to develop naturally in preschool children, and shows how these reasoning processes may run counter to the culturally determined, and more formal, logical approaches to knowledge that children are expected to acquire in school, particularly in mathematics and science. In a section dealing with language, Gardner describes how between birth and age 6 or 7, children become capable of "several ordered layers of symbolic sophistication." He outlines a number of stages of this development, all taking place before the age of 6. These stages take the baby from the "mundane" ability to "appreciate that words or pictures refer to entities in the world," through being able to employ symbols within a system (grammar), to appreciating that "symbols represent a point of view," and to recognizing that a point of view may "be contrary to the actual state of affairs." For instance, a child may know that a box contains pencils, but also understands that another person (falsely) believes that the box contains chocolates. As a result of this development, the 'average' 6-year-old "becomes able to appreciate that symbols represent a point of view, the mental state of the particular person who has issued the symbolic statement, " (p.97). These kinds of "second-order beliefs," said Gardner, enable children at the end of the preschool period to understand irony and sarcasm, such as somebody saying, "Isn't it a lovely day," when it is actually raining: "The speaker must know that the listener knows that the actual state of affairs is different from that which has been explicitly coded in the utterance" (p. 97).

CHILDREN'S THEORIES OF MIND

This kind of complex perspective-taking is called "pragmatic" in formal linguistics, and pragmatic understanding of "them" and "they" ("they're doing it that way to make you buy things") occurs frequently in the comments of the children in the study described in this book. All reconstructions of reality, as in art and media, presuppose another person's, or persons', point of view; television programs have been made by somebody, and one of the developmental tasks of the young child growing up with television is to work out who that somebody is, what they are up to, and why. Developmental psychologists refer to these kinds of thought processes as children's theories of mind, and a number of experimental studies have been done to discover what, in particular, preschool children's theories of mind are.

Surprisingly, very little of this literature uses children's everyday experiences of television consumption as a testing ground. Most of the work, as with a study by Adrienne Samuels and Marjorie Taylor in the *British Journal of Developmental Psychology* (Samuels & Taylor, 1994) uses print materials, picture books, or toys. These studies show developmental progression in the way children construct explanations about the phenomena in the world around them, including how real or how false they are. Using a task very similar to one of the tasks used in my Annenberg study, Samuels and Taylor asked children between the ages of 3 and 5 to identify whether a series of depicted events could happen in real life. They found that younger children had much more difficulty than older children in recognizing that, for instance, a moose cooking in a kitchen could not happen in real life.

There are problems with asking this kind of question of very young children because they may interpret the question idiosyncratically. Because of their difficulties with embedded thinking—thinking on more than one connected level—they may take the surface meaning and context of the question absolutely literally. They might, for instance, think that a picture of a moose cooking in a kitchen could occur in real life, because they had seen such a picture before. If they actually saw a moose cooking in a real kitchen, they would probably be as surprised as the rest of us. Samuels and Taylor acknowledged that such responses may have been an artifact of the question. If they had offered a forced choice—"Is this real life or is it pretend?"—the responses might have been different.

Samuels and Taylor's (1994) study also demonstrated interesting differences in response which may have been culturally induced. For instance, they found that, contrary to their prediction, children were more likely to be confused about the reality status of frightening pictures (taken from children's books), than of "neutral" pictures: "the tendency to claim that scary events could not happen in real life could be interpreted as a way of dealing with a negative emotional reaction to the pictures" (p. 425). It would be useful to know whether there was any relationship between this reaction and children's media experiences. Other studies, for example those carried out by Joanne Cantor and her colleagues at the University of Wisconsin (Cantor, 1994), showed that fear reactions to disturbing television material have a strong developmental component. Cantor proposed that, as a function of cognitive development, younger children respond to perceptible aspects of stimuli—surface features again—and older children respond more to conceptual aspects, or under-lying meanings. For example, Sparks and Cantor (1986) carried out a study examining children's fear responses to the TV show, *The Incredible Hulk*, in which a mild-looking young man is regularly transformed into a monstrous-looking, green-colored giant. The research found that pre-school children experienced most fear at the actual transformation. Older children in elementary school reported the least fear at this time, because they knew that the Hulk's transformation meant he was going to rescue some innocent victim and to restore moral order.

The complexity of this area of children's judgments about reality and fantasy is further illustrated by a study reported in the *British Journal of Developmental Psychology* in 1991. Paul Harris (1991) and his colleagues demonstrated that children up to the age of 7 or 8 were quite capable of understanding the concept of a fantasy, or imaginary animal, and they were able to test for themselves that imaginary creatures were not inside a box. However, they still showed reluctance to put their fingers into the box, in case their fingers were bitten by the animal.

THE POWER OF THE IMAGINED

Knowing that something is imaginary thus does not seem to lessen its perceived power. Adults who still shudder when thinking of nightmares will surely recognize this point. Indeed, it could be argued that, for children in middle childhood, trying to deconstruct or debunk the power of imagination, along the lines of Charles Dickens' Mr. Gradgrind, might be counter-productive. The ability to engage with emotional conflicts in mythical form through, for example, fairy tales, has been argued to be necessary to healthy psychological development by writers such as psy-choanalyst Bruno Bettelheim (1976) and novelist and folklorist Alison Lurie (1990). Hence, media education programs that seek to undermine the need to believe in fantasy and magic in children, particularly those under the age of 8, may be doomed to failure. Some evidence for this was produced by my Annenberg study, which found that first graders were significantly more likely than third or fifth graders to say that they believed that Santa Claus really existed. Several first and second graders also used the term *magic* as an explanation for television special effects, for instance:

> Int: How do you think they have him suddenly appear here?

> Jack(first grade boy): Maybe magic or a trick. Maybe they made a whole glass box but it was a mirror and you can see the guy.

LINGUISTIC DEVELOPMENT

As discussed briefly in chapter 1, the most universal form of symbolic processing, common to all human beings, is language. Linguistic structures and behaviors are demonstrated by babies from birth (see Davies, Lloyd, and Scheffler, 1987), and there is a strong case for believing that the ability to learn language is biologically innate (Lenneberg, 1967). Ochs (1979) pointed out the centrality of "pragmatics," that is, the ability to recognize that meaning partly depends on context, and on understanding other people's perspectives, in defining the functions of language for the developing child. With special relevance for my study (which is concerned with how children use formal cues in television to make judgments about programs' reality status), Ochs particularly draws attention to the importance of formal, grammatical characteristics in language in indicating "the child's increasing sensitivity to the perspective of the listener." As Ochs put it, "the child moves away from reliance on the immediate situational context . . . [and develops] the tense system, the use of articles, relative clauses, reference to entities in the past, future, or imaginary world" (pp. 12–13).

In this pragmatic approach to language, the forms of utterances, as expressed in their grammatical constructions, are not just internal linguistic rules put there to make life difficult. On the contrary, they act as stage directions for the successful performance of speech acts, both speaking and listening. Grammar tells the child what the context of other people's statements are, and what their points of view might be. A simple example is the young child's understanding of the articles *the* and *a*. Children learning to speak English in their second year of life hardly ever say "the" or "a." They say "want drink" or "dropped teddy" or "see car." But research has shown that children as young as 17 months can distinguish the appropriate use of "the" and "a" by other speakers. (Katz, Baker, & McNamara, 1974). Such research has demonstrated that young children can understand that the word "the" implies a shared knowledge between speaker and hearer and is thus different from "a." "*The* car" is a special car—our car, the one we both know about; "*a car*" is any car and does not imply any particular mutual knowledge. Thus, from the earliest period of communication, the child uses grammatical forms as cues to evaluate meaning, and to recognize the point of view of other people. Grammar is seen to have an essential social and communicative function.

As Ochs pointed out, "the most pervasive and fundamental speech act of all is that of reference . . . successfully accomplished when the speaker believes the hearer can identify what is being referred to." One of the earliest demonstrable acts of reference is pointing (see Davies, Lloyd, & Scheffler, 1987) for instance, when babies around the age of 7 months demonstrate that they are able to recognize that another person in the room can see the same thing that they can see. Similarly, one of the earliest one/two word sentences is "wassat?" By asking the question, the 1-year-old baby indicates that she understands that the other person is capable of answering it. She has a mental construct of the other person in the room as a partner in communication. Interestingly, too, the 1-year-old is unlikely to direct such a question at another baby. She seems to know that there are limitations on linguistic and referential knowledge in babies, but not in adults.

Here, again, a theoretical account of children's linguistic development links directly to the practical question of children's relationship to the mass media. All mediated representations are acts of reference, requiring the child to understand what is being referred to in a television story or message, but sometimes without the aid of the context and feedback provided in real life conversations. Ochs points out the important role of the adult caregiver in "making explicit background information that would go unspoken in adult-adult communication" (p. 16). An example might be the use of irony, as in the example already cited,—saying "it's a lovely day" when in fact it is raining. In televised information, the opportunity to check and double check the context and intention of an ironic comment is missing, unless it is done by another character within the script (a very useful source of media education for child viewers—more discussion about how television fiction comments on its own artifice is found in chapter 6). The provision of missing contexts suggests a positive function for media education.

UNDERSTANDING PERSUASIVE INTENT

Psychologist Brian Young (1984), in a paper about "advertising literacy", has proposed that any useful definition of media literacy must be related to linguistic development. Young argued against traditional developmental models of children's understanding, which are based too rigidly on the ideas of Jean Piaget. Piaget argued that there is a shift in cognitive processing from "preoperational thinking" to the ability to perform mental "concrete operations" at around the age of 7. Piaget demonstrated this shift by using conservation tasks. When asked to pour some liquid from a short fat container into a tall thinner one, children under 7 seemed unable to recognize that, although the shape of the container was apparently bigger, the amount of liquid was still the same; younger children argued that there was more liquid in the taller container. Older children were able to hold the two concepts in mind at once and to recognize that, however much the size and shape of one object changes, the volume of the other object—the liquid—cannot be affected. The concept of volume was conserved, an example of second-order or embedded thinking. (Piaget & Inhelder, 1968).

Young identified the pragmatic linguistic ability to recognize, for example, persuasive intent ("they're trying to make you buy their things") as crucial. For him, the key shift is toward this kind of second-order thinking, and the consequent ability to take another person's perspective. Young argued that, although this ability is certainly linked to the Piagetian idea of a change in children's thinking at around 6 or 7 years, the change has specific linguistic characteristics not fully acknowledged in the Piagetian approach. In Young's view, the comprehension of persuasive intent, or underlying reality, needs to be located, not in "a set of non-verbal procedures", (such as conservation tasks) but in "a theoretical framework where it has a natural affinity." For Young, this framework is contemporary linguistics, particularly "speech act theory, pragmatics and the understanding of illocutionary force." For a child to be literate, he/she needs to understand "the meaning of utterances and messages that take into account the context of the message and the intent of the communicator." (Young, 1984, p. 7-8)

METALINGUISTIC SKILLS

Other researchers provide some support for Young's views. Johnson and Pascual-Leone (1989), demonstrated that metalinguistic skills, such as the ability to understand metaphor, puns, ambiguity, synonymy, figurative language, and of particular interest to the present study, pragmatic intent, become more marked in middle childhood at around the age of seven or eight. Metalinguistic skill is the ability to use language to comment about language. The pun is one of the earliest and most obvious forms of this, as in the very old joke: When is a door not a door? Answer: When it's ajar. Very young children will not see the joke here, which resides in the fact that the words a jar have two distinct meanings: one, a container, and the other meaning "slightly open." In middle childhood such jokes are extremely popular, and they are another form of tribal currency in children's groups. The Opies (1959) provided a treasury of examples dating back to the early 19th century and beyond. They found punning riddles, such as "what has an eye but cannot see? Answer: a needle" or "what has teeth but cannot bite? Answer: "a comb" on packs of cards dated 1822. Rhyming riddles based on linguistic ambiguity dating back to the 14th century were collected by the Opies in Scotland. For instance, the following comes from a 14-year-old girl in Kirkcaldy:

A Bramble:

First I am as white as snow,
Then as green as grass I grow
Next I am as red as blood
Lastly I'm as black as mud.

THINKING ABOUT THINKING

Attaching the prefix *meta* to an intellectual process refers to the ability of the thinker to reflect on that process, to have some awareness of what he or she is thinking about, and how it is being done. In describing how the simpler thought processes of the preschool child yield to the more reflexive intellectual judgments of the older child, Howard Gardner (1991) referred to the development of metacognition. Metacognition helps us to evaluate the truth or falsehood of a statement and to assess the general reliability or unreliability of the information other people are giving us. In making such evaluations, metajudgments about form, context, and tone of voice are crucial. As with our earlier example of irony, the recognition of sarcastic intonation ("it's a *lovely* day, isn't it?") allied to the recognition of context (the fact that it is raining) are metajudgments. Metajudgments enable the hearer to reflect on the context of the statement and to decide on its "illocutionary force," that is, whether it can be trusted or not. The ability to make metajudgments about form, style, tone of voice, and context is clearly important for children in learning to evaluate the enormous variety of statements and representations confronting them through television and the mass media. Metajudgments are required while watching television in order to evaluate the reliability of its information, that is, how real it is. But what particular features of a television text stimulate metajudgments in children? My study was an attempt to find this out.

Because television has become so naturalized in everyday life, the kinds of judgments required to make sense of it can be taken for granted as simple and intellectually undemanding. In fact, they may require very sophisticated reasoning on the part of very young children. Moore and Frye (1991) referred to the ability to make attributions of intent and judgments about other people's mental states, as metarepresentation. Metarepresentation is a form of mental modeling of the representational process that requires the child to "think about *another's* [my italics] belief as false." In a phrase that mirrors the complexity of the thought processes it is describing, Moore and Frye describe metarepresentation as "representing a representation as a representation of reality, or, in other words, judging how the [*other*] person's representation relates to the world." (p.

4) Such a modeling process, requiring the child to formulate an idea about whether other people hold false opinions, is required in the process of evaluating the mental states of fictional characters as well as of their creators, although, again, the studies cited by Moore and Frye in their review did not refer to artistic representations. According to these studies, metarepresentation improves with age, but most of the work cited has been done with preschool children using controlled experimental tasks. Metarepresentation under these conditions seems well developed by around 5 years old. How children deal with the "falsehoods" of representational arts, as on television, is not addressed in Moore and Frye's review of theory-of-mind studies but it would seem a promising field for further research in this area. Two researchers who have applied linguistic models to the study of children's understanding of television are the Australian semioticians, Bob Hodge and David Tripp, whose work is described in the next chapter.

CRITICAL CONNOISSEURSHIP

In forming judgments about the realistic or otherwise nature of literary and artistic representations, readers/viewers have to make a critical judgment based, not just on a comparison between an artistic representation and the real world, but also on what they think the artist is trying to do. Readers/viewers/listeners have to construct a metarepresentation of the artist's goals and methods. Such knowledge requires an awareness that the work in question is a construct—something created by another individual - but it also requires us to be aware of the means the artist has used to bring about this construct, including his or her motives for doing so, and whether the job has been done well. These kinds of skills (commonplace requirements in the evaluation of literature or the arts, less commonplace in evaluations of popular mass media) are the skills of connoisseurship—the ability to appreciate, as well as to analyze. Such judgments also require a pragmatic sense of authorship (or auteur-ship) - a concept that may have been banished by French critical theory in the past 20 years or so, but is alive and well in the critical discourses of schoolchildren. The term they was used repeatedly by every one of the interviewees in my study. Six-year-old Joe's answer to the question, Who are "they"? was typical: "Um—the writers."

Generally, this kind of embedded mental processing (thinking about thinking, and thinking about other people thinking) has been shown to improve throughout the elementary school period (Gardner, 1991). However, as Buckingham (1988) argued, higher levels of processing may have to be developed at a young age in the processing of television material, which requires children from early childhood to follow complex narratives and to make pragmatic attributions about characters and events. This kind of knowledge is social knowledge, based on experience of interacting with other people—not only with mothers, who are traditionally (and narrowly) the focus of attention in the study of young children's emotional development, but also with fathers, siblings, other adults, and peers. Social knowledge is an absolute prerequisite of human survival. If young children do not interact with other human beings, their helplessness and immaturity for the first few years of their lives is such that they die. Children who live long enough to reach school age have learned, by definition, a great deal about other people. (See Richards, 1974, and Richards & Light, 1986.)

With my study, it was possible that no differences would be found between 6- and 11-year-olds in pragmatic references or the ability to think about other people's thought processes, including their desire to deceive. It was possible that 6-year-olds would have as many complex theories about social interactions, based on experience of life and of its mediated representations, as did eleven-year-olds. However, older children are likely to be more articulate and able to explain their judgments verbally. Although younger children cannot explain their reasoning in interviews, it does not follow that they cannot make sophisticated social and pragmatic judgments. Nevertheless, the definition of literacy adopted in this study included a linguistic, conversational response to questions of television reality, and it was expected that older children would demonstrate greater metarepresentational awareness than younger ones, as evidenced by their verbal expression of pragmatic judgments about production processes. This proved to be the case (see chapter 5).

PROSOCIAL REASONING

Children's pragmatic awareness—the increasingly complex linguistic and cognitive ability to recognize context, motive, speaker's intent, and potential impact—seems a fruitful line of inquiry for studying children's relationship with television for other reasons. It is an obviously relevant skill, if *literacy* is defined as the ability to enter the imaginative worlds of written literature and to understand how these worlds function. Pragmatic awareness is also implicated in prosocial reasoning and behavior. Eisenberg and Mussen (1989), in a review of theories of prosocial development, pointed out that determinants of prosocial behavior include: attributions, maturity, intelligence, the ability to see and evaluate the situation from the perspective of others (role taking, decision making, and moral reasoning.) Eisenberg and Mussen were careful to point out that, although being able to see another's perspective is a *necessary* condition of prosocial development, it is not a *sufficient* condition to produce prosocial behavior. It is obviously possible to have excellent insight into other people's motives and to use this insight for antisocial ends, as in psychological forms of torture. Nevertheless, the pragmatic ability to understand and attribute motives and to empathize with other people appears to be an important and potentially useful aspect of media literacy, not just for cognitive reasons, but also for the kind of prosocial reasons that concern educators and parents. This aspect of reality perception—the suggestion that it might be important in protecting children from feared antisocial effects of television—has stimulated a number of studies of children's understanding of televised reality, which is reviewed in the next chapter.

3

Reality Perception on TV

According to Robert Hawkins, who has done seminal research on children's understanding of television reality, reality perception must be seen not only as a useful critical skill, but also as an important defense against the harmful effects of television:

> If the social and psychological processes involved in television effects can be isolated, one can then search for ways in which those processes can be altered. . . .. Children's perception of television's reality has seemed an especially good candidate [for an intervening variable] and has stimulated much hope and considerable research. (Hawkins, 1977).

Other researchers, for example, Aimee Dorr and her colleagues (Dorr, Kovaric, & Doubleday, 1990), expressed similar hopes:

> The perceived realism of television content often plays a mediating role between exposure to television content and its social effects. . . . Many studies have shown that content perceived to be unreal or unrealistic has less influence on viewers' information, beliefs, attitudes, and behaviors than content judged to be real or realistic.

WHAT IS REALITY?

Underlying these concerns, but not made explicit, is an assumption that TV representations are never real, as measured against some unspecified standard of what *is* real. Questions of reality—or modality—are essential ingredients of media literacy and media education programs (see Brown, 1993), but in many such programs it is assumed that everybody knows what real is and, therefore, no definition is necessary. For instance, in a research project carried out by Morison, Kelly, and Gardner in 1981, children were asked to choose between a pair of TV/film representations and to say which is more real. Examples of such a pair was *The Wizard of Oz* in contrast to the news. The researcher already knew the "right" answer. The definition of reality here was seen as unproblematic; obviously the news was meant to be seen as the more real of the two. But this is only the case if reality is defined objectively as events that have reportedly taken place in real life, regardless of how these events are presented.

It is possible to represent real events in such a way as to make them seem like fiction, as my interviewees in the Annenberg study pointed out about a children's news item they were shown (see chapter 8). This raises the question of what Potter (1988) called "cues in the stimulus material" (p.38) and their contribution to judgments about reality status. A useful construct developed by Elliott and his colleagues (Elliott, 1983) is the idea of personal utility in evaluating how real viewers find televised representations. If personal utility is a criterion, then for young children *The Wizard of Oz* may very well seem more real (or relevant) than the news, in its mythic representation of childhood preoccupations and fantasies, such as abandonment, victimization, homesickness, friendship, and overcoming danger. So, although there is no doubt about the validity of Morison's findings—most children quite correctly identified the news as a more realistic genre than the movie—the inoculation argument that doubting its reality should lessen the impact does not follow. Knowing that *The Wizard of Oz* is less real than the news does not necessarily stop children from being really petrified, as my children were, by the flying monkeys. Such terror has never been provoked by the news, depressing and disturbing though it often is.

A more useful way of looking at this question where children are concerned is to ask, as Dorr and her colleagues (1983) did, what information should be taken seriously, and how do we identify it? The concept of taking something seriously avoids the existential difficulties of defining objective reality. It stresses the central teaching and socializing function of artistic and cultural representations. It emphasizes the necessity of adults helping children to tackle one of their central concerns: How do I know what or whom to believe? In other words, what could matter most for children when they try to judge representations of the real world, whether on television or anywhere else, is not how literally true to life these representations are, but how authentic they are perceived to be in addressing children's own concerns and preoccupations. This functional definition of *real* can also be helpful for parents: Realistic representations are accounts of human experience that they find useful in explaining how the world works to their children. Parents and other adults have always used a variety of myths and stories in carrying out their task of socializing the next generation. By this definition, *The Wizard of Oz* may very well seem to be more real—that is, personally useful—to young children than the news.

The Power of Fantasy

Fairy tales and fiction have traditionally been seen as the most useful forms of representation of experience for young children in their preoperational or premetarepresentational phase of development. Bruno Bettelheim's (1976) analysis of the meaning and importance of fairy tales is called *The Uses of Enchantment* (my bold), drawing attention to the fact that fantasy stories serve necessary psychological and developmental functions. Bettelheim argues that a fantasy tale like *Cinderella* symbolically represents universal childhood anxieties and can thus reassuringly address the psychological needs of children of both sexes:

> Every child believes at some period of his life . . . that because of his secret wishes, if not also his clandestine actions, he deserves to be degraded, banned from the presence of others, relegated to a netherworld of smut . . . . He hates and fears those others—such as his siblings—whom he believes to be entirely free of such evilness and he fears that they or his parents will discover what he is really like, and then demean him as Cinderella was by her family. Because he wants others, most of all his parents, to believe in his innocence, he is delighted that 'everybody' believes in Cinderella's. This is one of the great attractions of this fairy tale. Because people give credence to Cinderella's goodness, they will also believe in his, so the child hopes. And *Cinderella* nourishes this hope, which is one reason it is such a delightful tale. (p. 240)

Although Bettelheim is writing from a psychoanalytic perspective which is not universally shared by commentators on children's culture, this reading of one possible real meaning of *Cinderella* is persuasive. Literary critic and novelist Alison Lurie (1990) offered an even more robust defense of the realism of fantasy, as compared to the one-dimensional feebleness of much so-called relevant realistic writing for young children. She is particularly scathing about a book of stories that she was given as a child, which sought to be reassuring by describing mundane everyday experiences, rather than giants and witches:

> The children and parents in these stories [*The Here and Now Story Book*, by Lucy Sprague Mitchell] were exactly like the ones I knew, only more boring. . . . After we grew up, of course, we found out how unrealistic these stories had been. The simple pleasant adult society they had prepared us for did not exist. As we had suspected, the fairy tales had been right all along—the world was full of hostile, stupid giants, and perilous castles and people who abandoned their children in the nearest forest. To succeed in this world, you needed some special skill or patronage, plus remarkable luck; and it didn't hurt to be very good-looking. (pp. 17–18).

RESEARCH ON REALITY PERCEPTION

Nevertheless, despite authorities as eminent as the poet Schiller arguing that "deeper meaning resides in the fairy tales told to me in my childhood than in the truth that is taught by life" (quoted in Bettelheim, 1976, p. 5), many media education programs continue to be based on attempts to deconstruct the arts of television for children in order to arm them against its possible bad examples. Brown (1993), who provided the most extensive review of critical-viewing-skills (or media-literacy) programs in different countries, quoted the U.S. Parent Teachers' Association Commission on Television: "the trained viewer will recognize and avoid harmful effects of it [television]; and its unrealistic and stereotyped portrayals of individuals, groups, and lifestyles." (p. 96) According to the U.S. Education Office, also quoted by Brown, such training must include the acquisition of "primary viewing receivership skills" for elementary schoolchildren from kindergarten through grade 5 (the age group used in the present study). Such skills include, "distinguishing program elements such as music, special effects, setting, color, etc. . . . distinguishing fact from fiction . . . understanding style of dramatic presentations, public affairs, news, and other programming" (p. 96).

Because of this concern, particularly in the U.S., about the harmful effects of television and the belief that these effects can be mitigated by reality teaching, a number of studies have set out to examine children's concept of reality on television, with a view to influencing media-education programs. Most of these studies, as noted, rest on the assumption that there is such a thing as real-world reality, in contrast to the version of events shown on TV, and that real-world reality should be accepted by children as the preferred version. Indeed, a major theory of communication—cultivation theory—is predicated on the assumption that the real world has one set of reality characteristics and television has another, and that heavy viewers of television are more likely to believe television's version than the real thing, with negative effects. (Gerbner, Gross, Morgan, & Signorielli, 1980).

Hawkins (1977), in an influential paper, was careful, like other researchers, to describe the performances he is measuring as children's perceived reality. That is, children's judgments are defined as subjective—a matter of perception. In a study of elementary school children, Hawkins found four basic dimensions of reality perception:

1. Magic window reality (whether people are dramatic or actual people)
2. Children's expectations about life and the world around them
3. Specificity—answers depending on different types of show or characters

4. Context—the usefulness of people and events in everyday life (an earlier version of Elliott's personal utility construct).

In his discussion of Hawkins' work, Buckingham (1993a) reduced these dimensions to two: Magic window and Social expectations. These two dimensions, measuring, respectively, children's awareness of the artifice of television, and their use of their own experience to assess its plausibility, are similar to the dimensions of Art and Life used by Liebes and Katz (1990), which are discussed more fully in chapter 6. Most researchers in the field have thus found that modality judgments about the reality status of television (or of any other form) have two major sources: first, the formal characteristics of the text (Potter's "cues in the stimulus material"), and second, the reader/viewer's own experience of life as applied to what is going on in the text. In the case of children, the relative contributions of each of these sources also vary as a function of maturity.

THE SIGNIFICANCE OF MISPERCEPTIONS

Although children's perceptions of reality were the dependent variable in Hawkins' (1977) study, children's responses were still being implicitly measured against an adult researcher's ideas of objective reality: "dramatic or actual"; the world around them; everyday life. In a similar study to Hawkins', two Dutch researchers, Nikken and Peeters (1988), asked children questions such as "A child told me Tommie is put in a closet until the next *Sesame Street*. Do you think that is true?" (p. 450) Again, although it is the child's perceptions that are under investigation, the answer "no" has to be coded as wrong. Such questions are designed to uncover children's misperceptions, as measured against an objective standard of reality. *Why* the child thought that Tommie was not put in a closet was not fully explored, yet from an educational and literacy perspective, this seems pertinent. Nikken and Peeters also evaluated the children's ease of discussion in answering their questions, and this proved to be an "important [positive] predictor of the perceived reality of *Sesame Street*'s content." This finding suggests that literacy, at least in the sense of verbal expression skills, could be linked with literacy in its looser sense of "knowing the difference between TV reality and fantasy."

Other researchers, including Dorr (1983, 1990) and her colleagues, and Morison, Kelly, and Gardner (1981) explored children's reasoning processes about television reality in more depth. In Morison's study, as already discussed, children were presented with 12 pairs of programs, prechosen by the researchers, and asked to decide which were more real. In this forced choice task, children from second to sixth grade did not differ in their choices about which was more real. Nearly all made the "right" choices. Where children of different ages did differ was in the criteria they used to explain their choices. Morison (1981) found significant age differences in reliance on physical features—"art/magic window" criteria—as a reality cue, with 52% of younger children and only 15% of older children referring to them. This bottoming-out of references to physical features was also found by Hawkins (1977) and Dorr (1983). The question of whether younger children would be more influenced by physical features, in contrast to older children being more influenced by social reality considerations, is one of the questions investigated in my study.

Buckingham and his colleagues at the London University Institute of Education (Buckingham, 1993a) used a similar technique to Morison's, but without the limitations of having to make forced choices between pairs of programs. They offered groups of schoolchildren between 8 and 12 years of age, a list of 12 different programs, and asked them to put the programs in order of realism. They then audiotaped the resulting discussions. The children were also given lists of programs grouped by genre (family sitcom, soaps, children's live-action drama) and asked to discuss what made them distinctive. Buckingham found, as expected, that all age groups were very aware of the constructed nature of television, with wide-ranging discussion about different television techniques. He also found, as did Morison and Dorr, that there were progressive age differences in the kinds of cues used in making judgments about reality. Sixty-four percent of 8-year-old judgments were based on internal (or art/magic window) criteria; 36% were external (social expectation/life) judgments. Among 10-year-olds the proportions were 46% internal and 54% external, and among 12-year-olds, the proportions were 36% internal and 64% external. Girls were slightly more likely than boys to use internal (art) cues, and working-class children were much more likely than middle class ones to use them (60% working class to 43% middle class).

ART AND LIFE

Buckingham cautioned against reading too much into these figures, especially in view of the smallness of the sample. However, they do confirm the findings of other researchers that, as children get older, for whatever reason, they are less concerned with the formal trappings of television production as a way of assessing its reality status, and are more concerned with issues of plausibility and likelihood of content. Again, though, the relationship between internal, art-based judgments and external, life-based ones can be difficult to pull apart in some children's responses. Chapters 7–11 demonstrate that, with the interview subjects of my study, the two dimensions of art/magic window and life/social expectations could not always be separated, particularly in the judgments of more mature and sophisticated viewers.

Indeed, a major starting point for the study, supported by some children's comments, was that realistic judgments about the lifelikeness of television cannot be made without drawing on discriminating judgments about art. Here, for instance, is 10-year-old Lauren on the subject of music in the soundtrack of a children's fantasy drama, *The Sand Fairy*:

> Some music makes it suspenseful and it tells you when something exciting is going to happen. . . . This music is like hurrying and trying to get where they are going and they are trying to find things. It also helps you to get a feel of what's going on.

Lauren was not a musical child—"I don't play music"—but she made an intelligent aesthetic judgment about the quality of the music based on its rhythm and pace, allied with the action (children exploring an old castle). This judgment is intrinsically linked to her social-expectations judgment about the function of the music in underlining the action and also in leading the audience's expectations—"the music makes it suspenseful." She makes a number of pragmatic statements showing both awareness of the producers' intentions, and awareness of their impact on an audience: "It tells *you*"; "it helps *you*" (my italics). In this passage, Lauren's judgments about life (the events in the story, the characters' motivations, the producers' intentions, the effects on the audience) spring directly from her reading of the scene's art.

JUDGMENTS OF QUALITY

Morison and her colleagues (1981), in their study of children's reasoning about television realism, found that "contrary to expectation, critical consideration of the quality, authenticity, and veracity of television representations is rarely found, even among the oldest subjects" (p. 229). Thus, these researchers, in passing, raise a question that would be central rather than peripheral to any investigation of children's literacy if the subject were books. This question concerns the extent to which intrinsic qualities of the text play a part in the reader's interpretation of it. If children's responses to a poem, story, or drama had revealed a failure of "critical consideration of the quality, authenticity and veracity of . . . representations," (p. 241) there would be some concern that the children had not appreciated or understood the book properly. With television, for many researchers, there is no such concern. Buckingham (1988) commented on the contrast between the "impact mediation" approaches deemed appropriate for television literacy programs and the very different approaches to literacy and literature required by English teachers: "How often does one read English teachers arguing for the importance of rational analysis as a means of protecting children against the powerful emotional manipulation exerted by literature?" (p. 7).

Potter (1988), in a useful critique of reality definitions in research, was likewise critical of the tendency of researchers to know best and to define perceived reality as "a synonym for media accuracy . . . isomorphic to real life experiences" (p. 24). Potter laid special emphasis on what he calls "generational issues," arguing that they involve three important factors: (a) a person's experience with the media, (b) a person's ability to make sense out of media stimuli and (c) the type of cues in the stimulus material. "Cues in the stimulus material," Potter pointed out, have been "virtually ignored in the [research] literature" (p. 38). Such cues are a primary focus of the present study, whose object is to investigate media literacy in children.

If literacy is to be defined as more than a basic commonsense understanding of the difference between reality and fantasy, which develops of its own accord with age, then it seemed reasonable that an examination of media literacy should include responses to textual characteristics, as with books. It did not seem enough simply to ask children to make distinctions between reality and nonreality, which has been very effectively done by earlier researchers and was also done in the questionnaire used in my study. The study aimed to do more than to observe and count the use of different kinds of cues—internal (art-based) and external (life-based)—which, again, has been effectively done in a number of studies and is clearly linked with interesting questions of developmental progress. The goal of this study was to link children's reality awareness with specific formal features, to see if the grammar of the medium had the illocutionary force to direct children's readings and analyses of its meaning.

Not all internal cues have the same status. Informed critical analysis of a television drama, for instance, should be able to make distinctions between central questions of dramatic construction, which affect how convincingly a story is told, and more peripheral questions of, for instance, a character's hairstyle, which might be slightly out of period but would not affect the plausibility of the story. Both of these judgments are internal, to use Buckingham's phraseology, but one is conceptually central, the other relatively superficial. The goal of the Annenberg study interviews was to try to make distinctions between different kinds and levels of formal analysis, and analysis of the pilot transcripts did reveal different levels and types of judgment about the reality status of different production features (these are shown in chart form in Figures 5.1 and 6.1 on pages 54 and 77). In addition, pragmatic judgments about producers' intentions and intended impact on audiences provided a further dimension. Sometimes these pragmatic judgments were offered in answer to probes by the interviewers, e.g., "Why is it done that way?" But sometimes they were volunteered without prompting as part of the initial reality judgment, which suggests that children *seek* to make attributions about the purpose of different forms. For instance, 9-year-old Michael commenting on a commercial for Barbie-type dolls:

> I wouldn't want to see a commercial like that, as you see now, it makes them look like real people, or somebody really talking—"hey Ken"—and you know it's really the kids that are talking—uh, huh, and dressing them.

Michael's assessment of the nonreality of these dolls is based on his knowledge about the producers' intention to deceive—"it *makes* them look like real people." It is also based on his pragmatic awareness of his own distaste for such deceptions—"*I wouldn't want* to see a commercial like that"—and his own, and others', ability to see through them: "*You know* it's really the kids that are talking" (my italics).

MODALITY

The general label given to these kinds of judgments about reality, when they are based on production or textual features, is "modality judgments," and one of the most extensive accounts of media modality was given by two Australian researchers, Hodge and Tripp. In a study with Australian elementary schoolchildren, Hodge and Tripp (1986) made a comprehensive attempt to provide a theoretical framework that brings together social, educational, psycholinguistic, and literary concerns. Hodge and Tripp preferred the semiotic analysis of meaning systems and processes, and the intensely active process of interpretation to traditional methods of content analysis, which involve counting the frequencies of particular television representations, such as violent acts, or powerless women. Their objection to content analysis was that it "breaks up the meanings of a program or program type into countable units" (p. 5), and hence, fails to address more fundamental questions of symbolic, structural, and individual interpretation. Hodge and Tripp acknowledged the centrality of "reality and its definition" and its "continuing political dimension. . . . what children *ought* to think, not how things are." The name they gave to the features of a TV text which indicate its reality status is "modality." Perceived reality is a modality judgment based on formal characteristics of the material being read—in other words, a form of literacy; it is also another kind of metajudgment.

In Hodge and Tripp's definition, modality is "a linguistics term indicating the degrees of certainty of a sentence" (p. 70). In language, the statement "it's a monster" is weakened—in other words, its modality is lessened—when the statement is changed to "it may be a monster." According to Hodge and Tripp, fantasy is weak modality as long as it is recognized as fantasy. Hodge and Tripp connected with other researchers' concerns in stressing the role of formal features (that is, literary features) in facilitating modality judgments. They argued that children, by the age of 9, "use a large number of formal features as the basis for their modality judgments, distinguishing cartoons from films and films from real life." These judgments were made on the basis that cartoons look different from films, as films look different from real life. Cartoons, because of their unrealistic form, say "it may be a monster" rather than "it is a monster." For example, in a study of children's responses to a cartoon, *Fangface*, Hodge and Tripp identified a number of ways—drawing, two-dimensionality, special effects, the sheer unlikelihood of monsters going around an ordinary neighborhood—in which children identified the weak modality of the cartoon form, and thereby demonstrated media literacy.

Hodge and Tripp echoed thinkers such as Bettelheim in arguing the importance of yielding to imagination. They pointed out that the willing suspension of disbelief is a necessary response to a work of imaginative fiction, rather than an illusion from which the young need to be freed. Despite (or, as Hodge and Tripp would argue, because of) their ability to recognize the artifice of *Fangface*, the children in the study still enjoyed the story. Hodge and Tripp reminded us of Brecht's attempt to "distance his audience by . . . the alienation effect, which drew attention to the processes by which illusions were created, and thereby *raised* the audience's level of consciousness and powers of critical thought" (p. 104; my italics).

According to Hodge and Tripp, not only is it natural that people should temporarily believe in the fictional world of a story, provided this belief is based on the appropriate modality judgment, but it may even be desirable: "The belief that a work is literary leads you to cancel out your dominant modality system in the interests of a higher level of response, not a lower one."(p. 103).

The sophisticated thinking traditionally required of more advanced students of language and literature, Hodge and Tripp proposed, is now required of the very young by virtue of their constant exposure to and familiarity with the fictional forms of television. Hodge and Tripp's study suggested that young children are capable of this kind of literary judgment—provided they are asked the right kind of questions. Asking the right kind of questions is another potential function of media education.

UNANSWERED QUESTIONS

Hodge and Tripp have been influential in the thinking of other researchers into children's understanding of television, and *modality* is now a widely used term in discussions of people's readings of media. See, for instance Sefton-Green's (1990) discussion of different modality categories in his account of teaching about *The Cosby Show* (discussed further in chapter 8). Sefton-Green moved away from Hodge and Tripp's semiotic emphasis on specific formal features. Most of his examples involve the representation of social reality in comparison with children's real world experience; they include very little about production features as modality markers, not even broad and obvious ones such as genre. So, for instance, the fact that *The Cosby Show* is situation comedy rather than realistic drama was not considered relevant by Sefton-Green's interviewees in their discussion of its representation of race.

Hodge and Tripp's analysis of modality was primarily in terms of the drawn features of cartoons, and it left many interesting questions about other kinds of representations unanswered. To illustrate their analysis of modality, they discussed a still picture taken from a Batman comic strip; they pointed out that in the picture, three-dimensional features are strong modality, because they give a greater impression of realism; two-dimensional features are thus weak modality; realistic detail is strong modality; the alienating or weakening effects of print being included in the drawing are weak modality. All give cues to the reader/viewer about how to interpret the meaning and reliability of the picture, the relative power of the protagonists in it, and so on. In the case of cartoons, Hodge and Tripp challenge the idea that violent and scary cartoons have harmful effects on children; they claim that their study with children from 6 to 11 years of age demonstrated that cartoons' massive lack of realism—or weak modality—"turned something that would otherwise have been frightening into the opposite, something funny and/or exciting" (p. 112).

REALISTIC DRAMA

Other sorts of television—particularly realistic drama —do not offer such clear-cut opportunities for modality definition. Realism is strong modality and hence, realistic dramas as well as news and documentary (which have even stronger modality—or fewer modal transformations—on Hodge and Tripp's scale) have also given cause for concern to adults worried about young children's inability to distinguish reality from fantasy. The Hodge and Tripp study also raises the question already mentioned of whether all modality cues are equivalent, or whether some carry stronger indicators for judgment than others. As mentioned, questions of dramatic construction may be seen as more central reality cues than details of costume, or they may not. The children in Hodge and Tripp's study, as with Buckingham's, were all aware of performance. But would poor quality acting, as in the case of some soap operas, lower the modality of an otherwise convincing story? Performances, scripts, and production factors have different functions in realistic representations than in nonrealistic ones. One of the children in Buckingham's study, 10-year-old Anne, wittily parodied some of the problems of combining realism with regular doses of dramatic conflict in a continuing series about a secondary high school, *Grange Hill*:

> You're not going to go on demonstrations, and you're not going to feel so strongly and you're not going to fall in love with forty year old men, and you're not going to have weird teachers, and your teachers aren't probably going to change into different people, you're not going to suffocate yourself in an unventilated room with spray paint. . . (p. 229).

Discussing these questions in the classroom, as Buckingham acknowledged, is a way for children to distance themselves from the initial impact
of first viewing them. Emotion recollected in tranquillity is not a measure of
the impact of the material at the time—always a drawback of research, which
often discusses issues well after the event. This was one advantage of using
a technique in the present study which captured children's responses straight
away. (See chapter 6). Hodge and Tripp's defense of cartoons as being merely
funny because of their weak modality is strikingly similar to the inoculation
theory of media education: as long as you know it is not real, it cannot do
you any harm. But does modality judgment always necessarily work this
way? Does recognizing that something is somewhat over the top, as in Anne's
catalogue of disasters from the *Grange Hill* scripts, turn something that would
have been frightening into something the opposite? Other children interviewed by Buckingham suggest that the answer may be No. In discussing
Children's Ward, a children's drama series about a hospital, Buckingham's
subjects recognized the constructed and occasionally unlikely nature of the
events: "they locked themselves in the toilet . . . they wouldn't let them do
that in hospital." But it still expressed emotional reaction to them: "I just
think it's so revolting . . . with the operations. I'm not that keen on seeing a
lot of blood" (p. 231).

Hodge and Tripp suggested that, as with Brechtian alienation devices,
recognizing the constructed nature of art is actually a higher form of
response than being taken in by it. However, as already discussed, simply
recognizing that something is a construct does not necessarily lessen its
emotional impact, as with Paul Harris and colleagues' study about
children's fear of an animal that they knew to be imaginary (Harris,
Brown, Marriot, Whittall, & Harmer, 1991). Hodge and Tripp's defense
of cartoons in terms of their artifice so that potentially scary aspects seem
merely funny, is also not necessarily a defense of scariness. It might be
emotionally healthier, as Bettelheim argued in the case of frightening fairy
tales such as the Grimms' *Snow White* (where the wicked queen dances to
her death in red-hot iron shoes), for children to be really scared by the
story, as long as they are reassured by the justice of the ending.

The defense of finding horror funny also cannot be invoked in the case
of classical drama, which, as Aristotle pointed out, is *intended* to evoke
pity and fear through its artistic devices. I may know that *King Lear* is a
play by William Shakespeare, written in the distancing style of somewhat
archaic 17th century blank verse; I know that it is taking place on the
stage of the Barbican theater with Robert Stephens, whom I have recently
seen on film playing Sherlock Holmes, in the lead role of King Lear. All
of this knowledge weakens the play's modality. But none of it stops me
shedding tears at "Why should a dog, a horse, a rat, have life, And thou
no breath at all?" On the contrary, the simplicity of the poetry, the fact
that this is the culmination of Shakespeare's dramatic construction,
showing the decline of a powerful king into a pathetic bereaved father,

and the parallel transformation of the actor, seen as a handsome youngish man in the 1970s movie, into an enfeebled old man in the 1994 stage production, all add to the emotional effect.

THE RULES OF ART

This raises a question, which turned out to be quite significant in analyzing the comments of the children interviewed for this study: the question of internal rules of representation, based on a story's faithfulness to artistic norms, as well as to its relationship to the real world in generating modality judgments. If the norms of cartoons are violated by, for instance, introducing some real people (as in *Who Framed Roger Rabbit*, or in *Mary Poppins*), how are children's modality judgments affected? A very striking example of children's objections to a lack of reality in a program caused by a violation of internal generic rules was found in my study in response to a clip from *Sesame Street* (see page 86). This clip showed a cartoon of a man digging for treasure under a large T shape drawn in the sand. Several children, including the youngest first graders, objected that this was not real, not only because "there's no such thing as buried treasures," (and not at all because it was a cartoon), but "because it's usually an X." This judgment came, not from life, but from art; from their knowledge of the usual rules of treasure stories, where, as one 10-year-old succinctly reminded us, "X marks the spot." It was thus both a magic-window judgment, and a social expectations judgment, but here, the social expectations involved were internal ones drawn from the genre, not external ones drawn from life.

All the aforementioned studies found that responses to questions about reality or television representations varied as a function of age. Because, as Dorr described, virtually all children learn to recognize that TV reality is different from real-world reality by the time they reach adolescence, it could be argued that there is no need for educational intervention at all; in order to produce critical viewers, we simply wait for children to grow up. However, this gets us no further forward in understanding the mechanisms of children's understanding of and responses to TV—an important concern for developmental psychologists, for educators, and for parents. It also offers no theoretical explanations for the responses observed, and hence, no useful guidelines for drawing up media education curricula for children of different age groups, particularly the very young in whom reality perception has been identified as a problem.

In designing the present study, it was recognized as important to address two main issues. The first was to have a theoretical framework about children's understanding of media and real-world reality drawn from studies of child development, not just from communications or cultural theory. This framework should provide appropriate explanations for the particular behavior being studied—that is, children's under-standing of mediated representations, whether literal, symbolic, or a mixture of both. The most appropriate developmental framework for this purpose seemed to be cognitive, particularly language. In conjunction with this was children's theories of mind—that is, their ability to make judgments about their own and other people's mental states. Such judgments rely heavily on linguistic cues. The second issue was the importance of finding out what children's own definitions of reality or nonreality were, and what were their bases of judgment. The hypothesis of the study was that children would use formal features and codes of the medium as a basis for making modality judgments about the reality or nonreality, of television material. The questions were: Which features and which codes? How and why would children's judgments vary?

4

Formal Features, Literature, Art, and Education

The present study, like virtually all others on the subject of media literacy, concerns itself with reality perception and, as such, asks questions about children's ability to tell the difference between reality and fantasy. However, following Hodge and Tripp's analysis of modality as the key to evaluating television's reality status, the emphasis in this study is on the role played by the medium's formal features in generating these judgments. Such an approach brings the study of children's readings of television closer to more traditional ideas about literacy drawn from books. Modality judgments, as described by Hodge and Tripp, are a form of literary analysis; they require viewers to make principled appraisals of the forms and techniques of the medium in order to make inferences about meaning and about the relationship between represented events and real-life ones.

FORMAL FEATURES

Formal features of television have been widely studied by North American researchers, in part stimulated by the extensive formative research for *Sesame Street* carried out in the 1960s, which showed that the attention of preschool children to the screen was a function of a variety of formal and stylistic aspects: music, editing, sound effects, animation, and so on. (Lesser, 1974). The attention-getting function of production features is well known and, thanks to increasingly sophisticated technology, special effects and stylish graphics have become a standard feature particularly of commercials and, increasingly, even of news production, partly, no doubt, as a result of these early findings on *Sesame Street*. The attention-getting function of special effects was well recognized by the young subjects of my study. Asked why they thought the producers used unrealistic production features, the answer "to get your attention" was by far the most frequent. However, the formal features of film and television, as with those of grammar and literature, not only direct attention; they also direct the interpretation of meaning.

Film theorists and practitioners such as Eisenstein (1943) and Metz (1974) have long described film as having its own grammar. Developmental psychologists have attempted to determine whether the formal features of audiovisual media can be described in ways analogous to language, with implications for how children make sense of these media. In an introductory chapter in *Children and the formal features of television* (1983), Rice, Huston, and Wright summarized the main aspects of television's representational codes. They identify three levels of representation: First, as with Gardner's account of linguistic/cognitive development (see page 11), there is the simple referential level, "the literal visual and/or auditory portrayal of real world information, e.g. a shot of a car moving on a highway" (p. 24). Second, there are media forms and conventions, which they describe as "analogs of perceptual experience", such as camera cuts and zooms, and the use of fades and dissolves to indicate time passing or the end of a sequence of events. The third level of TV's formal features identified by Rice and her coauthors consists of "symbolic forms not unique to the medium" such as complex verbal language or the use of other visual codes such as red traffic lights. These kinds of codes can be used to enhance TV-specific codes, as when, to use Rice's example, a fade is accompanied by the line, "Once upon a time, a long time ago." (p. 24)

The research carried out in my Annenberg study was particularly concerned with the second and third levels described by Rice and her colleagues, that is, the extent to which TV's codes and analogies act as grammatical guides to judgments about the reality and reliability of the content. Exact analogies between linguistic grammar and film and television grammar have been attempted by a number of theorists, such as Kraft (1986) and Carroll (1980); other writers are skeptical that there is any kind of meaningful parallel between written and film grammar. Buckingham, (1993a), for instance, emphasized literacy as a set of social, rather than individual skills. His work with discussion groups of children suggests that meanings are negotiated within "interpretive communities," to use Stanley Fish's term (Fish, 1980). However, an individual's ability to read and write—to decode commonly-held systems of written language—does not preclude the same individual also being part of an "interpretive community." On the contrary, Buckingham's social literacy does require some minimal level of personal understanding of symbolic codes as a precondition of joining the interpretive community in the first place.

This is as true of being able to read and write as it is of what Bianculli (1992) called "tele-literacy." Individuals who lack the skills of reading and writing are excluded from the community and, in the case of print illiteracy, can suffer severe social and economic handicaps as a result. Such handicaps do not at present afflict the non-tele-literate, partly because knowing about television is not seen as particularly culturally valuable in our society, and tele-literate individuals are not considered to be in possession of specialized skills. As cultural capital, to use Bourdieu's term (1984), tele-literacy has a fairly low market value. This may change, as television becomes, like film, superseded by new forms of leisure activity, such as computer games, and the fans and lovers of the medium come to be seen as the guardians of rare, specialized knowledge, that may be in danger of dying out. This process is showing signs of happening now. Already Roseanne has had the accolade of one of *The New Yorker's* extended literary articles devoted to her (Lahr, 1995).

HUMAN SYMBOLIC FUNCTIONING

The interesting questions for a psychological inquiry concern the mental processes of those doing the reading. Given that human symbolic functioning is very diverse and adaptable, it is possible that the processes by which the young mind learns language can also be adapted to learning the codes of television. If this is the case, the ways in which children make sense of television may be able to shed light on their ability to handle other symbol systems, such as print and speech. Children are exposed to speech from birth, and most children in the industrialized world are exposed to television almost as soon. Children learn their own native spoken language from being surrounded by it; it is possible that they learn the codes of television by an analogous procedure, although, as already mentioned, television does not give the same feedback as live caregivers do. The linguistic and symbolic information provided in mediated experiences has to be yet further mediated by other people. There is certainly evidence that children learn more from the medium when parents watch television with them (e.g., Salomon, 1977). This suggests that a closer parallel for learning from television may not just be with spoken language, but with learning to read. Children at first need the mediation of adults in order to connect the printed symbols on a page with meaningful messages. Then they learn to work it out for themselves.

Adults do not need to teach children to make sense of television, so critics like Neil Postman (1985) suggested. However, his assertion was based on no empirical evidence about the way families watch television; the fact that children do seem to learn to read television effortlessly does not mean that no teaching is going on, any more than the fact that children appear to learn to speak effortlessly means that they have received no help from others. As Bianculli's book documents, and as family studies like Salomon's in Israel and Palmer's in Australia (Palmer, 1986a & 1986b), suggest, tele-literate children have both literate and tele-literate parents who help them to see the connections between TV, books, theater, and real-world experiences.

ACTIVE AND PASSIVE SENTENCES

If reading television does have parallels with reading (or processing) other kinds of media, including language, whether spoken or written, then we would expect some of the forms of television to be analogic to the forms of linguistic structures. Research carried out for my PhD thesis indicated that Rice's idea of editing as a "perceptual analog" could apply to linguistic structures such as simple active and passive sentences.

I used some television sequences from a preschool children's program in which there were two versions of the same simple action. One version was shot in medium shot and uncut; the other started with a medium shot and then had a cut to close-up, emphasizing the object (or patient) of the action. In the uncut version, a sequence showing a woman lifting a toy chair without any cutting to close-up was an analog of the active sentence "The woman lifts the chair." The whole event was seen in medium shot and the most prominent person in it was obviously the woman. In the passive version of the sentence, "The chair is lifted by the woman," the chair is foregrounded. The visual analog of the passive form was a medium shot of the woman lifting the chair followed by a close-up of the chair.

Normally, people recall the agents of actions better than the objects they are acting upon. However, this is not the case with passive sentences, which put the object in the foreground and make it more memorable. As with recall of passive sentences, the people taking part in my research who saw the cut-to-close-up version were more likely to remember the chair than to remember the woman. The opposite was the case with the uncut version. (Davies, 1988). The structure of the visual sequences thus seemed to parallel grammatical linguistic structures in viewers' minds.

METAPHOR, METONYMY, AND CONNOTATION

Rice and her colleagues further propose that this analogic level, in which television codes model linguistic ones, includes connotative devices such as music in a minor key for suspense or fast editing and high levels of action to connote gender—as in ads for boys' toys. These connotative devices have come to be seen as part of the conventions of the medium and nowadays are taken very much for granted, but they have not always been so. They had to be invented by early directors and film editors, and then they had to become normalized by professional use. Connotative uses of media conventions have strong literary parallels. They can be metaphoric, in which, to take the example of gender representation, the use of speeded-up motion in a film sequence represents the energy of a boy taking part in a race. Here, to use the literary phraseology, the boy is the topic of the metaphor, the fast camera movement is the vehicle that expresses his energy, and the speed that they hold in common is the common semantic ground of the metaphor. Work on children's understanding of metaphor has been done by Janice Johnson and Juan Pascual-Leone in York University Ontario (1989). As we might expect from both cognitive developmental and linguistic theory, their studies showed that younger children find it more difficult than older children to understand the appropriateness of metaphoric relationships, probably because, as with conservation tasks, more than one level of meaning has to be held in mind at once.

Film and television's connotative devices can be metonymic (or associational) as well as metaphoric. In the case of metonymy, a fast cutting rate does not necessarily have any intrinsic relationship with boyhood (many boys are slow and lazy), but if it is used sufficiently often in programs aimed at boys, it will eventually come to connote boyness by association. Similarly, slower cutting rates, soft focus, pastel colors, and romantic music are not intrinsically girl-like (many girls are energetic, noisy, fond of bright colors and fans of rock 'n' roll). But if used often enough in conjunction with programs and products aimed at girls, they can eventually be used entirely by themselves as visual shorthand for femininity. This is one of the ways in which critics of the medium argue that television has a socializing, or even a brainwashing effect in creating stereotypical attitudes. Such conventional and unnoticed techniques may be cultivating ideas in children about what appropriate gender qualities are supposed to be (boys are energetic, girls are sweet and gentle) without their being aware of it.

Teaching children to understand how visual editing may be used in these literary ways must be a part of media literacy education. But, as with other kinds of literary techniques (metaphor and metonymy have been socializing human beings since the invention of lullabies and the first use of toys), this literary approach does not have to espouse one set of interpretive values over another. Connotative devices, like rhetorical and poetic ones, are used for emphasis and aesthetic effect, but unless you agree with Plato in deploring all kinds of poetic exaggeration, they are not necessarily and automatically suspect. Metonymy may influence in many kinds of ways, including propaganda. But the influence of a text, or story, is not just a function of the writer's, director's, producer's or polemicist's literary conceits. As many modern critics have pointed out, the viewer/reader plays a central part in interpretation, too.

SCHEMAS AND TRANSFORMATIONS

In his book, *Actual Minds, Possible Worlds*, psychologist Jerome Bruner (1986) wrote an account of his and his colleagues' attempt to reconcile literary theory and analysis with actual psychological processes in real readers. He pointed out that when readers were asked to tell back a story, different readers did it in different ways, according to their preferred schemas of interpretation:

> "Telling back" a Conrad story, one reader will turn it into a yarn of adventure, another into a moral tale about duplicity, and a third into a case study of a *Doppelganger*. . . . If we then ask about the nature and role of *psychological* genre—the reader's conception of what kind of story or text he is encountering or 'recreating'—we are in fact asking . . . a question about the interpretive processes that are loosed by the text in the reader's mind (pp. 6-7) [Bruner's quotation marks and italics].

Bruner described some studies with readers in which he was able to demonstrate that grammatical transformations—linguistic forms that express context—had a central function, not only in enabling the writer to suggest the point of view of the characters in the story, but also in enabling readers to interpret the author's meaning and to make inferences about the characters in the story beyond what was specified by the author. In retelling the story, readers used even more transformations than did writers in trying to express their sense of different points of view. For instance, here is the first sentence of the short story, *Clay*, by James Joyce, and then its retelling to Bruner by a teenager:

> Joyce: The matron had given her leave to go out as soon as the women's tea was over and Maria looked forward to her evening out.

> Teenager: The story goes like this: Uh, he starts out by uh, telling us that, um the lady named Maria will be um waiting for, is waiting for the women to come for a tea party type of thing. (p. 161).

Joyce's sentence takes us straight into the story from Maria's point of view; we know that Maria is going out that evening. Assumptions about who the matron' is, and what the women's tea might be, have to be made by the reader, but we are given some help about the plot. We know that Maria is going out that evening. The teenager provides further transformational perspectives; for a start he points out that somebody is telling the story to somebody else—"he starts out by, uh, telling us"—and he then helpfully implies that Maria is an invented character who had to be given a name by the writer—"the lady named Maria." He then continues with the story. As often with retellings, the teenager uses the descriptive present tense (as I am doing here); he is describing what somebody else has *said*, not actual events. The original omniscient narrator, on the other hand, uses the past tense; the impression is that he is recording real events that have already happened. These different kinds of linguistic modality markers indicate the level of reality and reliability of the information, through what they reveal about the point of view of the teller, and his or her distance from the reported events.

As one would expect if the interpretation of television stories is seen as similar to literary analysis, there were a number of examples of retelling by the interview subjects in my Annenberg study that showed similar constructions and attributions. For instance, third grade Elijah, speculating on the children in *The Sand Fairy* who have been magically transported to a medieval castle, explained:

> The kids got there somehow and something is happening to the village and they want to know what is happening. Because they're bringing all these soldiers to stop somebody.

Elijah changes from the past to the present tense to indicate the "kids'" point of view; it is from their perspective that something is happening. From his own perspective as narrator, which is how he starts, something has already happened. The "they" who are "bringing all these soldiers" is not the "kids" but some assumed absent authority, whom Elijah has not seen, but he is inferring that somebody must be responsible for the sudden appearance of a troop of knights in armor. *The Sand Fairy*, as a fantasy story using magical special effects, was a very good example of how such stories can be used to encourage children to "subjunctivize"—to use Bruner's term—to create their own interpretations, using the conventions and techniques of the medium as cues. Fantasy, as expressed in formal techniques unique to television, such as characters suddenly appearing and disappearing, is a particularly fruitful incentive to this kind of speculation.

Elijah illustrates Bruner's argument that readers "subjunctivize" when they read a text—that is, they go beyond the information given to try to construct their own "virtual texts," based on their interpretations of what the author might mean (a linguistic modality judgment), what the characters might be feeling, and how this relates to the reader's own experiences and expectations. The act of reading, for Bruner, involves all these mental activities. Good literary writing, as practiced by a master such as James Joyce, is the kind of transformational writing that enables these networks of possibilities to be set up in the reader's mind. Bruner did not refer to nonliterary texts, such as films or television programs, although he might well have done so.

Another educational writer and researcher, Susan Neumann of Temple University, did concern herself with television, and used rather similar techniques to Bruner's in studies described in her book, *Literacy in the Television Age* (1991). She argued that the interpretation of television stories is an active process, with many similarities to reading printed text. For her, the common element to both processes is the activation of "schemata" or mental scenarios based on the reader's expectations and knowledge, which guide the viewer/reader's processing of a series of events as they unfold. The activation of schemata is the true function of reading:

> In sharp contrast with prior notions of reading as a linear process consisting of aggregating the meanings of words to form the meaning of clauses and then sentences, comprehension is seen as a matter of activating or construct-ing schemata that provide a coherent explanation of objects and events mentioned in discourse. (p. 73)

Schemata, according to Neumann, could include knowledge of genre and of the normal conventions of different kinds of programs, as well as knowledge of life drawn from experience. Obviously, the younger the child and the less the child's experience of both art and life, the fewer the schemata available to be activated—or the less literate the child. Neu-mann describes an exercise with her son in which she asked him to comment on what is going on in a children's detective story, and she observed how he gradually seemed to be activating a particular schema to interpret it—a MAGNET schema (Neumann's uppercase letters). David used his understanding of magnetic force fields to work out how the mystery in the story would be solved, once he was told that the girl detective was going to expose a fraud by using a compass. At every stage in the story, he was anticipating how a magnet might be relevant to the action. Since the action concerned some con-men trying to pass off an ordinary piece of rock as a valuable "white dwarf"—"matter condensed beyond the wildest imagination"—David was able to use the MAGNET schema to work out how this trick could be exposed (p.85). Bruner's and Neumann's studies demonstrate that concepts drawn from literary analy-sis and cognitive psychology, such as story schemata and linguistic transformations, provide models for understanding how the mind might organize information coming from stories and how this information can be used to make inferences and attributions about wider motives and values, including the relationship of the story to the real world.

PRAGMATIC PERSPECTIVES

In Rice's model of representational codes (Rice et al., 1983), the second-order pragmatic level of inference and attribution is not explicitly dis-cussed. The pragmatic level requires children to be aware of context, authorship, and audience effects; to have a sense of agency. They need to realize that, to use Rice's example of how fades in film indicate time-pass-ing, someone made a decision to fade to black, and someone wrote the sentence "Once upon a time." Pragmatic knowledge also enables the viewer to be aware of how the fade works on an audience: "It makes you feel that we're going back in time." This level of decoding—the level of literary or artistic connoisseurship—turned out to be prevalent in the interview subjects of my study. These audiovisual representational codes, or formal features, although very different in many ways from linguistic grammar, seem to require somewhat analogous cognitive structures and procedures in children's thinking. We have seen that language develops from simple referential statements to subtle pragmatics as children use increasingly complex linguistic forms to express their relationship to the world around them. Similarly, it can be expected that children's ability to use their developing powers of symbolic processing to make sense of other representational codes, as on TV, would also develop with age and experience.

LITERATE VIEWING

The Israeli developmental psychologist, Gavriel Salomon, was one of the first to use the term "literacy" to describe the processes involved in making sense of audiovisual information (Salomon, 1979). Salomon used the term "literate viewing" to describe the "process of information extraction by the active negotiation of the coding elements of the message" (p. 189). Salomon, too, is one of the rare researchers in this field to make detailed reference to the arts, especially the visual arts, in his analysis of what it takes to be medialiterate. His book, *Interaction of Media, Cognition, and Learning* (1979), contains detailed accounts of art theory and film criticism in its analysis of television's and film's representational codes, which, he pointed out, are multiple, complex, and interacting. They include images, movement, music, print, spoken language, and camera techniques, usually operating simultaneously.

To appreciate fully what is going on in an audiovisual text, the viewer/listener has to have an understanding of each of these different codes and has to be able to integrate them into a unified narrative. The present study, in its emphasis on the decoding of televised material as a form of literary analysis, rather than as a clinical diagnosis of harmful effects, follows Salomon in seeking to integrate cultural, arts-based approaches to the study of the media with the more systematic analysis of audience responses as practiced in the social sciences. This integration is difficult, but it is required of all of us who work in media education, whether at the college level, as I do, or in elementary and high schools, as other media educators do (see Davies, 1996). A good media-studies syllabus needs to draw on the insights of the creative arts; cultural studies; social, political, and psychological analysis; as well as on professional and technological practices.

These last have not been much reviewed in the various effects and media literacy studies discussed in earlier chapters. However, the educational value of production in teaching analytical and critical skills is becoming increasingly recognized as modern technology—inexpensive camcorders, CD ROMs, computer packages of various kinds—make creative media work for children in the classroom more feasible. Watson (1990), who has written about the educational use of film and television production, speaks of his own training as a filmmaker as a "model of humanistic education." Other production teachers have described methods of imparting creative skills that generate intellectual activities, such as decision making, cooperation, and literacy (e.g. Viglietta, 1992; Newell, 1995). Production is a recognized part of a number of exam syllabuses in secondary (high) schools in Europe. As Viglietta's work in Italy illustrates, it can also be integral to the training of teachers, not only for media education, but also in other areas such as science. As different forms converge into multimedia computer packages that can be used educationally, more students will technically be able to handle diverse media forms—images, text, and music—for their own learning purposes (see e.g., Laurillard, 1993).

CURRICULAR THEMES

In Britain, along with production techniques, the differing levels and accounts of decoding or reading the media, have been translated into curricular themes that are fairly widely used in media education. These accounts provided a useful basis for analyzing some of the data in the present study. In *Primary Media Education*, (Bazalgette, 1988), six curricular themes are identified:

Agencies

Categories (or genres)

Technologies

Languages

Audiences

Representations

In her monograph on media education for the series *Teaching English in the National Curriculum* (1991), Bazalgette, one of the authors of *Primary Media Education*, combined these groupings into three:

1. Media languages (What does this text say? How does it say it? What sort of text is it?)
2. Producers and audiences (How was the text produced? By whom and why? For whom? How did it reach its audiences?)
3. Representation (Judgments about truth/authenticity/accuracy/realism. Judgments other people might make. What does it represent?)

The last-mentioned element, What does it represent?, is in Gardner's and Rice's analysis of encoding, the simplest—or lowest—referential level of processing: identifying an object such as a car on a highway. Representation is sometimes taken to have more complex levels than this, particularly when social judgments are being made. For instance, a car driving along a highway in the context of an ad for a luxurious Rolls Royce, may be seen to represent wealth, or even ostentatious wealth, incorporating morally judgmental schemata. These are connotative judgments, higher order inferences operating at a more complex level than the mere recognition of a vehicle on a road. To a baby, or to someone lacking WEALTH or LUXURY CAR mental schemata (to use Susan Neumann's capitalization), the car on the road is likely to represent just a moving picture of a big shiny car. For a baby, even ROAD schemata may be lacking and only the car will have any representational salience.

Judgments about representations also raise questions about Bazalgette's list of truth/authenticity/accuracy/realism. These judgments, too, move the child's thinking about this car onto a more complex level, in which features specific to the medium help to answer "how" questions. How is the impression of a car driving along a highway achieved? How convincing an impression is it? Answers to these questions produce references to formal features such as editing, framing, sound effects (engine noises, tires screeching, etc.) Children may also, if prompted, use "how" questions to draw wider inferences about the connotative associations of wealth and the luxury of the Rolls Royce. This level of judgment also involves Bazalgette's (1988) category of media languages: "How does it say it?"

Questions about producers and audiences (Bazalgette's third group) are, in Gardner's developmental account of symbolic processing, at the highest level; other sorts of judgment are embedded in these judgments, and hence they are "second" or "higher-order" processes. They require pragmatic awareness of context, motive, attribution of intent, and empathy with other people's points of view. Because they are more complex, and also require greater world knowledge, they are more likely to be found in children aged 8 and over, as Young (1984) suggested. These kinds of judgments involve awareness of connotation, allusion, semiotic signification, authorial intent, and aesthetic impact. They require children to activate schemata based on knowledge of other sorts of representation, such as stories and pictures, as well as on real-world knowledge. As Neumann pointed out, the fewer the available schemata in a child's mind, the less able the child is to make sense of different sorts of representation and the various formal features that characterize them. The less mature, the less knowledgeable, and the less tele-literate child will be less competent in constructing what Bruner called virtual texts: meaningful interpretations based on what the author appears to be meaning, as well as what the author is actually saying. This is where tele-literacy overlaps with other kinds of literacy and knowledge.

DEFINITIONS OF GENRE

The media languages question, "What sort of text is it?" is partly a question about genre—a very prominent area of study in film and cultural studies, and one that turned out to be important for my child subjects in deciding what was real and what was not. (For instance, animation was not seen as unreal in the context of a program for preschoolers, such as *Sesame Street*, but was seen as unreal in a news item.) From the point of view of metacognitive processing, genre is a higher-order inclusive category, which requires the child to organize referential and structural information into larger classified categories according to some kind of systematic principles of grouping. Not only critics, but also producers and program schedulers have increasingly rigid definitions of different genres: soap opera, Western, thriller, psychological drama, *film noir*, and so on. These categories are defined—usually by critics, sometimes by producers—according to narrative, design, and performance characteristics. They are also increasingly defined by assumptions about their target audiences. These assumptions translate into marketing decisions: for instance, certain kinds of material are pitched at different kinds of audiences, and are screened in different places or at different times of the evening, depending on what genre they are judged to be. Thus, sitcoms are shown on TV in prime time, horror films late at night. However, the principles of classification used by the media industries and by critics are not necessarily the principles that operate in audiences' judgments of these products.

In a study with 9 and 10-year-olds in Bristol, England, educationists Eke and Croll (1992) asked the children to arrange different kinds of programs (listed by themselves) according to their similarities and differences. Although they were given opportunities to generate answers such as soap opera and quiz/game shows, they never did. The most frequent constructs for grouping programs offered by these children were:

1. Humor: "funny"; "makes you laugh"; "comedy" etc.
2. Excitement: "lots of action", "people fighting" etc.
3. Involving children: "children in it"; "no adults"; "it's mostly children," etc.

Even the ubiquitous cartoons were not grouped together as cartoons, but under the heading of "funny." The construct "containing children" was particularly striking in this study—it incorporated a wide range of different genres, including a children's quiz show, an adult quiz show, the school drama *Grange Hill,* and the magazine information program *Blue Peter*. Eke and Croll's study demonstrated very clearly that "linking program format with understanding . . . [tends to] rely on adults' distinctions of program type and adult-identified markers of plot information" (p. 98). Adults' categories were not seen as useful to children when it came to making category choices of their own.

Although Eke and Croll's study was not directly concerned with reality/fantasy distinctions as my Annenberg study was, their findings underline quite forcefully the importance of understanding children's definitions of the formal and other features of television texts and not using adult definitions, whether of genre or of the modality markers of represented reality. Hence, the methodology of my study needed to allow children to make their own judgments about what was and was not real and why, and to find reasonably naturalistic ways of enabling them to do this.

5

The Sample and the Study

AIMS AND DESIGN OF THE STUDY

This chapter describes the aims, design, sample, procedures, and statistical results of the Annenberg Media Literacy study. The chapter deals primarily with the first part of the study—the questionnaire data. The next chapter discusses the design and methodology of the second, interview, stage. The study was concerned with modality judgments, that is, the extent to which children use formal features of a text to assess its reliability and its relationship to their own sense of the real world. Modality judgments based on formal features address all the key questions about media interpretation identified in Bazalgette's account of primary media education: representation, language, technology and categories. Judgments about agency (producers' intentions) and audiences (judgments about likely viewership and impact) arise out of these formal judgments, and, in my study, are classed as pragmatic.

The study used both a conventional questionnaire format and a qualitative interview procedure, and was carried out on children between 6 and 11 years of age. This is the age group identified by Brian Young and other developmental psychologists during which relevant and significant cognitive and linguistic developments occur. During this period, children's theories of mind, that is, their judgments about the nature of reality, fantasy, fact, and opinion both in themselves and in others - which are related to these metacognitive developments, become increasingly sophisticated. It is also a period when television watching is popular and when children are capable of making their own discriminating choices about what they like, rather than having their viewing primarily guided by parents or other adults. The reasoning and opinions produced are thus more likely to be their own; it was also important, for the interview group particularly, that the children should be capable of having an articulate conversation with an adult they did not know. Elementary school children are more capable of this, and also more used to it, than are preschoolers. Hence, the choice of age group.

QUESTIONS ADDRESSED

These are the five main questions addressed in this study:

1. To what extent is reality/modality judgment related to age and development?
2. Is there any difference between children's reality judgments about TV and other kinds of reality judgments?
3. To what extent do children use formal cues as a basis for judgments about TV reality, and what are these formal cues?
4. Are these judgments related to other kinds of metalinguistic skills, for instance the ability to understand metaphor?
5. Are these literacy/modality judgments related to prosocial judgments?

METHOD AND SAMPLE

Two methods of investigation were used: a questionnaire administered to 82 children between 6 and 11 years of age, and an interview protocol with a subset of 18 children in the same age range, based on their responses to excerpts from four different television programs shown to them on a videotape at the time of the interview.

The subjects were 43 girls and 39 boys from two schools in a middle-class neighborhood of Philadelphia. Studying children of only one social class raises obvious problems of external validity, which limits the generalizability of the findings. In a small scale, short-range study like this one (the Annenberg Fellowship was for six months), there is no real answer to this problem. The sample had to be an availability sample from two schools who were willing to allow the researchers to come in. The principals were favorably disposed to the study, and once parental consent had been obtained via letters home, no obstacles were placed in the way of carrying out all the procedures involved in the research design: interviewing, questionnaire administration, use of school equipment such as VCRs, and information and advice about the children's reading levels from an extremely helpful school librarian. Even so, this was still a time-consuming procedure and most of the data analysis had to be completed after the end of the Fellowship period.

Nevertheless, because one independent variable of the study was age, the use of a homogeneous group of children with similar social and educational backgrounds meant that age differences could be isolated relatively easily, without confounding influences from class. Further, the use of availability samples of children is not unprecedented; it is a standard procedure in much developmental psychology research, which uses, for instance, university nurseries as a source of subjects. In working with children, ethical considerations obviously make it important to operate with consent from the children (who need to feel comfortable), from their teachers, and from their parents. Hence, availability is a crucial factor in obtaining access to willing participants in research with children.

The other mitigating factor in defense of the study's sample is that television stands virtually alone as a common cultural experience for all children, with middle-class children and working-class children having similar experiences of the medium and many favorite programs and consumption patterns in common (see Tables 5.4 to 5.7). The favorite programs of the children in this study correspond fairly closely to the programs that are generally most popular with child audiences in the U.S. according to Neilsen ratings, as do the children's self-reported patterns of viewing. Hence, in terms of their television-consumption, these children were not untypical of the child audience as a whole. The qualitative part of the study—the interview material—like all qualitative research, makes no claims to universal applicability, but it offers the research advantages, as summarized by Wimmer and Dominick (1991), of being naturalistic, flexible, and in depth. Like other qualitative research, it is seen as a starting point for further investigations.

AGE RANGE

The ages of the children ranged from 6 to 11 years. The boys came from first, third, and fifth grades; the girls, although their age ranges were the same as the boys', were distributed slightly differently between first, second, third, and fourth grades. Because the age ranges were the same, and because age and grade were very highly correlated (.95), the second grade girls were included with the first graders and the fourth grade girls were included with the fifth-grade boys, to yield three age groups: first, third and fifth grades. As with all age groupings, these were somewhat arbitrary, but it allowed the age groups to be sufficiently large for age-related trends in the responses to be identified. There were 15 boys in first grade, and 13 girls in first/second grade; 11 boys and 14 girls in third grade, and 13 boys in fifth grade and 16 girls in fourth grade.

THE QUESTIONNAIRE

The questionnaire was produced in two forms: a pictorial form for first and second graders (Appendix A) and a written form for third, fourth and fifth graders (Appendix B). The questionnaire was piloted with a number of children of acquaintances and colleagues, between 4 and 11 years of age, and adjustments were made for comprehensibility and length. The school principal and class teachers checked the questionnaire beforehand for its literacy level and appropriateness for their pupils, and no changes were required. Both the written and the pictorial versions had six main groups of questions:

1. Demographic information, including age, gender, school, and information about TV viewing, liking, and favorite programs. It also asked about other media use, including exposure to video cameras, VCR, reading, and whether family members worked in the media.

2. Multiple choice statements requiring the child's opinion: (true/not true/not sure) about television reality, for instance, "TV shows like *The Cosby Show* and *Full House* happen in somebody's real house" (REALTV). Children scored 2 for correct answers (in this case, not true); 1 for not sure and 0 for incorrect (in this case, true). Answers had to be coded as correct or incorrect since sometimes "true" was the right answer, and sometimes "not true" was.

3. Multiple choice questions about non-TV reality beliefs, for instance, "Santa Claus is a real person who brings us gifts." (REALIFE).

4. Open-ended questions about technical effects, for instance, how they thought the pictures changed on TV. These produced some interesting answers, including drawings one of which is reproduced in Fig. 5.2 later in this chapter. Many younger children were not able to answer these open-ended questions, because they required reasonable writing ability.

5. Questions about TV designed to show awareness of metalinguistic forms such as punning, for instance, a question about why the Count in *Sesame Street* is called the Count (METALING).

6. Questions about the morality or immorality of, for instance, showing realistic violence or deceptive commercials on TV (PROSOCIAL), for example, "It's OK to show violence in programs on TV because it makes the programs exciting."

The Interview Material

For the 18 interview subjects, nine boys and nine girls, three from each age group, a videotape was prepared of four short clips from *Sesame Street*, *Real News for Kids*, *The Cosby Show*, and *The Sand Fairy*, as described in chapter 6. These excerpts were recorded on VHS videotape and played to each child individually on the school's VCR. Children were asked to hold the remote control and to pause the tape "whenever they saw or heard something that couldn't really happen in real life." An interview protocol was then followed to explore their reasons for pausing the tape. The interviews were recorded on a RS Micro-27 cassette recorder.

PROCEDURE

The questionnaires were given to the children in small groups in a play or seating area outside their classrooms. With first and second graders, the experimenter read the questions aloud and the children circled the appropriate responses. They were not able to answer fully the open-ended questions, that relied on writing, but many of the younger children were able to write some simple responses, including the books they had recently been reading.

The interviews were carried out one on one, in a small room outside the classrooms, made available by the schools.

PREDICTIONS FROM THE QUESTIONNAIRE

The following predictions were made:

1. Correct answers to REALTV and REALIFE would be significantly more likely with age because reality perception is widely believed to be a function of development (Dorr et al., 1990).

2. It was hypothesized that scores on REALTV and REALIFE questions might not be correlated, because reality perception has different dimensions (c.f. Hawkins, 1977). Other research on children's perceptions of TV reality has not cross-checked for non -TV misconceptions that young children may have (see Harris et al., 1991).

3. METALING would increase with age and it would correlate positively with reality perception measures.

4. PROSOCIAL would correlate positively with reality perceptions, because an ability to tell fantasy from reality is seen as a defense against antisocial effects (Dorr et al., 1990). No age or gender predictions were made about answers to PROSOCIAL questions; however, differences were observed, particularly as a function of gender (See Table 5.3).

No predictions were made about the relationship between TV use, TV taste, and performance on the above dependent measures. However, in line with Gerbner et al.'s (1980) theory that heavy viewing is correlated with a variety of negative effects, viewing hours and liking for TV were compared with other variables, and some significant relationships were observed.

No predictions were made about gender differences, but all measures were compared as a function of gender, and some significant differences emerged.

PREDICTIONS FOR INTERVIEW MATERIAL

The interview material was qualitative, designed to elicit children's own judgments about TV reality or nonreality in their own words. It was predicted, from pilot interviews using the protocol, that children would notice many instances of TV unreality, but that these might vary as a function of program genre. Obviously, because of the task, all of these instances would be based on some aspect of the TV material's formal features, whether narrative, structural, or stylistic effects. It was hypothesized, in line with Morison's (Morison et al., 1981) findings, that older children would be less affected by purely physical features and would base their judgments more on plausibility (what would happen in life). Because the focus of interest was children's use of 'modality' the material was coded in two ways:

1. What kind of response caused the children to pause the tape. These responses are described in chapters 7–11, together with a more detailed account of the program features that produced the responses.

2. An analysis of everything the children said subsequently, in terms of the references they made to different formal features. These broke down into a number of modality judgments, which, as would be predicted from the theoretical developmental accounts produced by Gardner (1991), Rice et al. (1983), and Young (1984), were based on different levels of complexity, from the simple referential to the complex pragmatic. These different kinds of modality judgments are itemized in Figure 5.1 (overleaf).

RESULTS

Questionnaire Findings

Overall, children of all age groups showed good awareness of TV illusions, with 92% knowing that Superman and Batman cannot really fly, 75% knowing that TV fights are not real, and 78% agreeing that TV ads make items like toys and candy look nicer than they really are. However, fewer than half—47%—agreed that TV sitcoms took place on sets, not in real houses. This suggests that the naturalistic style of family shows like The Cosby Show, or Full House, is an important reality cue, despite obvious artificial elements, such as the laughter on the soundtrack. (See the interview data for further elaboration of this point.)

There was a distinction between knowing that TV is unreal and the more mature ability to make a moral judgment on these deceptions. The figure for, recognizing the falsity of ads (78%) is much greater than the proportion of children (45%) who thought that deception in ads was "not OK," even in order to sell the goods.

Results of Predictions

Age and reality perception.   Mean scores for the three different age groups in their awareness of real world illusion (REALIFE) are shown in

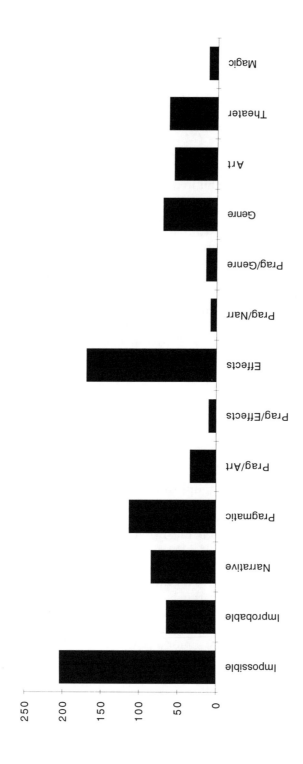

FIG. 5.1. Interview transcripts: Number of modality references, by category.

Explanation of terms used in Fig. 5.1.

LIFE CATEGORY: Referring to real-world experience

1. Impossible: Could not happen at all (violation of physical laws).
2. Real/Improbable: Unlikely to happen in real life (usually applied to human behavior).

ART CATEGORY: Referring to production features

3. Narrative: unrealistic in terms of story (e.g., "there's obviously something going on . . . but she doesn't notice it.")
4. Pragmatic: "They do it that way to get your attention."
5. Pragmatic/Art: "They put the music there so it helps to know what's going to happen."
6. Pragmatic/Effects (Fx): "[On montage] you can get people from all over the world and tape them."
7. Effects: "They're doing something with the camera—to make it go fast."
8. Pragmatic/Narrative: "They're doing it that way [double jump] so she can do the part where she says 'king me, king me.'"
9. Pragmatic/Genre: "This is a program for preschoolers who are learning the basics."
10. Genre: "A fairy tale—something that is not true—the way the child stayed up in the air . . ."
11. Art: "They're just trying to make it look better."
12. Theater: "Those sets in the background don't come with it."
13. Magic: "The future has real good magic things."

Table 5.1. (Means represent marks out of 2, since 2 was the maximum score for each question.) Independent T tests produced a highly significant difference between first and fifth grade for REALIFE questions ($t = -2.7$, df.55, $p = .009$) and a nearly significant difference between fifth and third grade ($t = -1.86$, df. 52, $p = .069$). The difference between first and third graders was not significant.

Mean scores for awareness of TV illusion (REALTV) across age groups are shown in Table 5.2. On REALTV questions, the most marked age difference was between fifth and third graders ($t = -1.83$, df. 52, $p = .072$) but no other differences approached significance. Interestingly, the mean was higher for the first/second graders than for the third graders, though not significantly so.

Relationship between REALTV and REALIFE.   There was no significant correlation between the answers on these dimensions.

Hence, these results show some improvement in reality perception with
age, but no strikingly significant differences for increasing perception of
TV reality. There is, however, a strikingly significant difference between
younger and older children for the REALIFE questions.

METALING Scores.   METALING scores (anchor and count) were
comparatively few, disappointingly, and produced only a weak positive
correlation with reality measures. More data points would be needed to
test this relationship more effectively.

PROSOCIAL Scores.   PROSOCIAL scores were not significantly correlated with either of the REALITY measures; a positive correlation here
might have lent some support to the inoculation hypothesis, with children
who were more aware of television illusion showing more disapproval of
it. However, this was not the case.

There was a highly significant gender difference on the PROSOCIAL
measures, with girls giving a much higher proportion of prosocial answers
than boys ($t = -.273$, d.f. 80, $p = .008$). The means are shown in Table
5.3.

In a two-way crossed ANOVA (gender x age), on the PROSOCIAL
scores, gender was significant at $p=.005$, $F = 8.363$, and age made very
little difference ($F= .932, p = .450$).

In the smaller group of interview subjects, there were some significant
relationships between PROSOCIAL and PRAGMATIC scores, which
suggests that the ability to perceive producers' intentions is linked with
prosocial awareness, as hypothesized.

In the whole group there was no significant difference between age
groups on the PROSOCIAL questions, although older boys performed
better on it than younger boys, whereas girls did not differ much across
age groups.

TABLE 5.1
Mean Scores for Awareness of Real-World Illusion (REALIFE)
According to Age Group

	1st/2nd Grade	3rd Grade	4th/5th Grade
Mean score	1.178	1.320	1.621

TABLE 5.2
Mean Scores for Awareness of TV Illusion (REALTV) According to Age Group

	1st/2nd Grade	3rd Grade	4th/5th Grade
Mean score	1.607	1.400	1.724

TV and other media access according to gender and age.

1. 94% of boys and 92.5% of girls had a VCR at home.

2. 64% of boys and 62.8% of girls had a video camera at home.

3. 28% of boys and 22% of girls had programmed a VCR. In girls, VCR programming was significantly more frequent with age (chi.sq., p=.0438); this was not the case with boys. Nearly as many first (35.7%) as fifth grade (39.3%) boys had used a VCR; with girls, only 18.2% of first graders had, compared with 31.8% fourth/fifth graders. Programming a VCR also significantly correlated with heavier viewing (Pearsons r .3104 p . < 01).

4. 66% of boys and 55.8% of girls had used a video camera. This was significantly more frequent with age in both groups (boys, chi sq. p = .0069; girls, chi sq. p= .0284).

5. Very few of the children had parents or household members who worked in the media: three of the boys (7.7%) and six of the girls (14%).

TV viewing according to gender and age.

1. Table 5.4 shows the distribution of viewing frequencies for boys and girls. There were no significant differences between them, but there are more heavy viewers among boys than among girls.

2. Table 5.5 shows the distribution of viewing frequencies according to age and gender ("Infrequent" is grouped scores from the "very little" and "sometimes" categories. "Frequent" is grouped scores from "often" and "very often" categories). None of the differences is significant, but there is a trend toward more heavy viewing with age for girls, but not for boys, where the largest number of heavy viewers occur in the first grade.

3. Table 5.6 shows the distribution of liking TV for boys and girls.

4. Table 5.7 shows the breakdown of liking scores across age groups, grouped into nonlikers ("Not much") and likers ("a lot"). This shows a very small decrease in boys, and a small increase with age for girls.

5. There was a highly significant positive correlation between TVWATCH (viewing hours) and TVLIKE (liking TV; r .7038, p. < 001).

TABLE 5.3
Difference Between Boys and Girls on PROSOCIAL Questions: Mean Scores.

	Boys	*Girls*
Mean score	0.794	1.325

TABLE 5.4
Viewing Frequency in Boys and Girls (%). Base 39 Boys, 43 Girls

	Never	A Little	Sometimes	Often	V. Often
Boys	0	5.1	25.6	30.8	38.5
Girls	0	14	37.2	18.6	30.2

TABLE 5.5
Frequent and Infrequent Viewers According to Age and Gender (%)

	(Infrequent)		(Frequent)	
	Boys	Girls	Boys	Girls
1st grade	10.25	13.95	28.2	4.65
3rd grade	10.25	20.93	17.94	11.62
5th grade	10.25	16.27	23.07	20.93

TABLE 5.6
Liking TV According to Gender (%)

	Hate It	Don't Like	Don't Mind	Like	Like a Lot
Boys	0	5.1	0	23.1	71.8
Girls	0	7.0	11.6	32.6	48.8

TABLE 5.7
Liking TV According to Age and Gender (%)

	Not Much		A Lot	
	Boys	Girls	Boys	Girls
1st grade	0	0	30.76	16.27
3rd grade	5.12	6.97	15.38	9.30
5th grade	0	0	25.64	23.25

Relationship between TV and other media use, and Reality, Metalinguistic and Prosocial measures.   There were significant correlations between:

1. TV watching (heavy viewing) and VCR programming (r .3104, $p < .01$).
2. There was a significant negative correlation between TV watching (heavier viewing) and PROSOCIAL scores ($r = -.2996$, $p < .01$).

There was no significant correlation between TV viewing, TV liking, and the reality and metalinguistic measures.

Favorite programs.   Children were asked to list their favorite programs, and some children mentioned more than one. Boys mentioned 23 programs and girls 18. There was a considerable spread of shows mentioned, with only a few shows attracting more than five votes.

1. Favorite show for all children was *Full House* (11 votes, 3 first-grade boys, 1 first, 1 second, 3 third, and 5 fourth-grade girls.)
2. Favorite show for boys was *Ren and Stimpy* (5 votes, 3 first graders, 2 fifth graders).
3. Favorite show for girls was *Beverly Hills 90210* (8 votes, all fourth graders.)
4. Other shows liked by both boys and girls were *Saved by the Bell* (10 votes); *Home Improvement* (4 votes); *Fresh Prince of Bel Air* (3 votes); *Hey Dude* (3 votes) and *Unsolved Mysteries* (2 votes).
5. Other shows receiving a single mention ranged from *Square One TV* (Children's Television Workshop's math program) through *Married with Children* to sports for boys, and from *Carmen Sandiego* through *The Young and the Restless* to *Star Trek, the Next Generation* for girls.

Answers to open-ended questions.   The questionnaire concluded with an open-ended question that gave children the opportunity to express modality awareness in their own written words. This question was: "How do the pictures change on TV?"

Sixty-six of the 82 children answered this question: 39 girls and 27 boys. The children who did not answer either left the space blank or, in a few cases, had to go back to their classrooms before they could finish. Hence there were only 13 first graders (3 boys, 10 girls). There were 25 third graders (14 girls, 11 boys) and 28 fourth/fifth graders (15 girls and 13 boys.) Two children produced drawings (see Figure 5.2, p. 63).

The answers broke down into four main groups:

1. References to the camera
2. References to animation—paper drawings, flip books, etc.
3. Other miscellaneous references, such as references to changing the scenery. In this group were a couple of references to satellite technology.
4. Don't know.

It was difficult to generate meaningful age differences with these responses, particularly because so few first graders answered. The largest number of references to cartoons and animation came from first grade girls (5) and, intriguingly, more third-grade than fourth-grade girls referred to cameras (5 third-grade, 2 fourth-grade). The largest group of "don't knows" were from fourth-grade girls (9). Age differences are shown in Table 5.8.

There was a striking and consistent gender difference in these answers, as Table 5.9 shows. This suggests greater interest in technology among boys. The age differences (though caution is necessary because of the lack of first graders) suggest the curvilinear relationship observed by other researchers, such as Hawkins and Dorr, where references to technological features peak in middle childhood and then become much less salient as modality markers as adolescence approaches. But in this sample, this curve only appears in the girls. Fifth-grade boys were more technology aware than third graders. Ten out of their 13 explanations—77%—referred to cameras, video technology and editing, compared with 6 out of 12 references—50%—in third grade boys. Among girls, 5 out of 14 third graders (35%) talked about technology, compared to only 2 out of the 15 fourth graders (13%).

SUMMARY OF MAIN FINDINGS FROM THE QUESTIONNAIRE

1. There was a significant increase with age in REALIFE scores with older children much less likely than younger ones to believe in mythical figures such as Santa Claus, or to believe that wishes come true.

2. This was not the case with REALTV scores, where, although older children performed better, they were not significantly more likely than younger children to be aware of TV artifice.

3. Overall, children of all age groups showed good awareness of TV illusions, with most knowing that special effects and theatrical settings were not real.

Table 5.8
Differences Between Age Groups for Explanations About How the Pictures Change on TV (% of Children Giving References)

	Refs to Camera	Refs to Animation	Other	Don't Know
1st/2nd Grade	31%	38%	0%	31%
3rd Grade	44%	12%	24%	32%
4th/5th Grade	42%	6%	17%	35%

TABLE 5.9
Differences Between Boys' and girls' explanations for How the Pictures Change on TV (% of Children Giving References)

	Refs to Camera	Refs to Animation	Other	Don't Know
Boys	60%	8.5%	19%	12.5%
Girls	22%	20%	12%	46%

4. There was a distinction between knowing that TV is unreal and the more mature ability to make a moral judgment on these deceptions. More children were able to detect unreality in TV than expressed disapproval of TV deceptions.

5. Girls were significantly more likely than boys to score highly on the prosocial questions. Gender was a much more significant factor than age in high-scoring prosocial judgments. The same distinction was found between the much smaller number (28%) of boys, compared with 60% of girls, who disapproved of deception in ads.

6. Heavier TV viewing was significantly correlated with lower scores on the prosocial questions. this was not accounted for by the small differences between heavier viewing between boys and girls, which were not significant.

7. Metalinguistic awareness was not significantly correlated with the reality measures. As mentioned, the data points would probably need to be increased and the questions refined to test this more effectively.

8. There were slight age differences in awareness of technology in the group of 66 questionnaire respondents who answered, as measured by their explanations of how the pictures change on TV. But there was a much greater difference between boys and girls, with a majority of fourth-grade girls answering "don't know," in contrast to third-grade girls, where over a third gave technology-based answers.

DISCUSSION OF THE QUESTIONNAIRE FINDINGS

An unambiguous finding from the questionnaire stage of the study was the very significant difference between younger and older children in their real life, non-TV beliefs about Santa Claus and birthday wishes coming true. Younger children, on the whole believed, and older children emphatically disbelieved (with third graders agnostically in between). On the other hand, the measures designed to test the children's understanding of TV reality showed no statistically significant differences between age groups. Time-honored adult assumptions, such as the belief that children believe they can fly like Superman, found almost no takers at all in this group. Similarly, most children knew that fights in television adventure shows did not hurt people, that TV ads made things look nicer than they are, that news anchors are not by themselves in the studio; older children knew that *The Cosby Show* is produced on a set and that programs are paid for by producers, advertisers, and media corporations. These children did not have media education in school, but nearly all were familiar with the medium and with its hardware (VCRs, camcorders), watched it regularly, and liked it quite a lot. They were also primarily middle-class children with other sources of information about the media, such as trips to Disneyland (although hardly any had media workers in their immediate households).

PROSOCIAL AWARENESS

The inoculation hypothesis (that awareness of TV illusion should have some kind of morally protective effect) predicted a relationship between REALTV scores, i.e., awareness of TV illusion and PROSOCIAL scores, i.e., disapproval of the use of illusion to glamorize violence or to sell products. However, the small positive correlation found between these scores was not significant. Instead, an unpredicted, but age-old protective factor turned up in the questionnaire results, namely, gender. A striking finding of the data was the superiority of girls over boys in answering prosocial questions. Indeed, to the extent that the boys tended to give more technical detail in their open-ended answers and to have more experience with camcorders and VCRs, the study even provides some tentative evidence, which needs further exploration, that there might be a negative correlation between technical awareness and prosocial attitudes, although no negative correlation was found in the main analysis. Younger girls were more likely than older ones to talk about technology in their open-ended answers. An example of an 8-year-old girl's ideas about How pictures change on TV is given in Fig. 5.2.

The drawing shows a viewer with a remote control sending "radio wavs" (sic) to the TV set; both viewer and TV set, interestingly, are drawn in profile, an unusual choice for children's drawings, which tend to be full frontal (Krasny Brown, 1986). Below the viewer, whose position is therefore dominant, is the wider context of media production: the TV station, with people (stick figures in this case, in contrast to the more salient viewer) at the control panel. Emanating from the TV station are "the channl" (sic), directed toward the TV set, and some unspecified waves directed toward what look like telegraph poles on the highway. On the left of the drawing, and uncharacteristically (for children) small, is the house, perhaps the home of this viewer, or perhaps a more generalized representation of "the home."

This rapid sketch demonstrates a very sophisticated understanding of the complex set of relationships between technology, producers, viewers, and society at large, on the part of the young artist—all in answer to the superficially simple question about editing: "how do pictures change?" It demonstrates another fruitful way of exploring children's understandings of media, apart from talk and writing.

PROSOCIAL JUDGMENTS

The PROSOCIAL questions required some fairly subtle moral thinking and were designed to test children's ability to make attributions about motive to other people (in this case TV producers) and to pass judgment on those motives. Hence, they required pragmatic, second-order reasoning, which younger children tend to find more difficult. The questions

FIG. 5.2. "How the pictures change on television." Drawing by 8-year-old girl.

63

were phrased as "It's OK to make toys in ads look nicer, so that kids will buy them" or "It's OK to show violence on TV, because it makes the programs exciting"—classic rationalizations offered by the industry whenever they are criticized on prosocial grounds. Girls were far more likely than boys to disagree with this rationalization, and, as expected, older children were more likely to disagree with it than younger ones—boys as well as girls. However, gender was a more powerful source of difference in these judgments than was age. There were few other gender differences, apart from some differences in viewing patterns and choice of favorite program. The fact that a gender difference turned up in prosocial judgments suggests work that could be done by classroom teachers in being aware of and working with different moral perceptions in boys and girls of this age.

The need to reach and please audiences can be the basis of many different kinds of media education work, particularly in language and the expressive arts. How far do you go without compromising integrity? Media education theorists such as Alvarado, Gutch, and Wollen (1987), pointed out the difficulty of teaching political economy and institutional aspects to young children. However, my study suggests that children, particularly girls, can form strong views about issues that are of direct relevance to them, such as advertisers cheating them.

More support was provided for another popular cultural pessimism hypothesis, namely the relationship between heavy viewing and negative attitudes identified by cultivation theory. Prosocial scores were significantly negatively correlated with self-reported heavy viewing ("I watch TV very often"). This did not appear to be a gender affect, because boys and girls had similar heavy-viewing scores. The sample was too small for multivariate regression analysis to be meaningful, but a larger sample could help to identify which factors (e.g., TV viewing habits or gender) make most difference in prosocial judgments, such as disapproval of media manipulation. This study's results favor the view that being female overrides the contribution of heavy viewing.

METALINGUISTIC ABILITY

In line with Brian Young's hypotheses, the study hoped to find some relationship between children's handling of metaphor and allusion (in the metalinguistic questions about the meanings of *anchor*, and the Count in *Sesame Street*). This relationship did not appear, possibly because there was a number of missing values in the youngest groups.

STATISTICAL ANALYSES OF INTERVIEW DATA

The interview data is primarily qualitative, and a detailed analysis of the children's comments, which were eloquent, imaginative and revealing, is found in chapters 7–11. However, some quantitative analyses were possible with some of the data. Correlations were run between the reality measures from the questionnaire and the interview subjects' modality scores (the number of references made to modality features) to look for relationships between them. Positive correlations were found between the following:

1. "Toy Ads are OK" (one of the PROSOCIAL questions) and the number of pragmatic references in all the interview children ($r. 6938$ $p. < 01$)
2. Pragmatic scores and combined PROSOCIAL questionnaire scores ($r. 687 p < .01$)
3. Pragmatic scores and age ($r .4819 p < .05$).

All modality references of any kind were combined for each child, and T tests were run between age groups on these combined modality scores. There was a significant difference between first and fifth graders ($t = 2.39$, d.f. 10, $p = .038$). There was also a significant difference between first and fifth graders on pragmatic scores ($t = 2.94$, df 10, $p = .019$) and a nearly significant difference between third and fifth graders on pragmatic ($t = 2.1$, df 10, $p = .062$). As with other researchers there was an age difference in the salience given to effects, but the difference between first and fifth graders in this study was not quite significant: $t = 1.53$, df 10, $p = .157$.

These analyses support the metalinguistic developmental theory that second-order pragmatic judgments are partly a function of age. Where modality judgments are concerned, the findings also suggest that metal-inguistic maturity is not just (if at all) a matter of knowing the difference between reality and fantasy, but more the ability to infer other people's motives and to comment on them. Although the interview group was small and the results should therefore be treated with caution, the observed relationship between pragmatic references and PROSOCIAL judgments is consistent with the view that it is necessary to be able to take other people's perspectives in order to adopt mature moral positions (c.f. Eisenberg & Mussen, 1989). This also reinforces the need for the kinds of media-education programs, such as those proposed by Jerome & Dorothy Singer, that foster imaginative play (Singer & Singer, 1976).

The questionnaire results, as already acknowledged, cannot be completely generalized to children of all classes and ethnic backgrounds. However, they do support some, though not all, of other researchers' findings about developmental progression, and they do generate some further questions for research. It was against the background of these findings that the second qualitative phase of the research, the interviews, as carried out. The questionnaire phase had followed the standard researcher's procedure of assuming, in James Potter's words, that the researcher "knows best", and that "perceived reality" is "a synonym for media accuracy, isomorphic to real life experiences" (Potter, 1988, p. 24). In other words, for the sake of acquiring reliable quantitative data, the questions put to the children had right/wrong answers; the "correct" answer to "*The Cosby Show* takes place is in a real house" is "Not true" Answers were coded accordingly: 2 for "Not true," 1 for "Not sure," and 0 for "True." However, a major goal of the study was to look at children's own understandings of the meaning of the word *real* and to trace the influence of television's formal and stylistic features in helping them to make modality judgments. This required a more qualitative approach. Attempts at naturalistic assessments of viewers' experiences of television, especially children's experiences, raise interesting methodological difficulties, which are discussed in the next chapter.

6

The Interview Methodology: Recognizing the Not Real

In their study of how viewers from different cultures interpreted the TV show *Dallas*, Liebes and Katz (1990) drew attention to the problem of methodology: "Ideally we should like to have empirical data on how people interact with their television sets *under natural conditions* [my emphasis] . . . how they decode what they see and hear" (p.20). For Liebes and Katz, behavioristic studies showing what viewers do, or what they say they feel while they watch TV, (c.f. Kubey and Csickzentmihalyi, 1990), "cannot explain the ways in which viewers use the program to comment upon life and upon art" (p. 20).

One problem for research lies in the interpretation of the word *natural*. What *are* natural conditions for investigating how people decode television? The very idea of analyzing their own thought processes about popular entertainment can provoke strong resistance in viewers (Dyer, 1992), and it could be argued that there are no natural conditions for such investigations. Any research project asking people to reflect on their own interpretations of the media runs the risk of either antagonizing viewers or putting them into an artificial situation in which they are less likely to tell the truth. For these reasons, some researchers, such as Buckingham (1993a), have expressed skepticism about talk data. As he said, "Researchers have tended to take talk at face value: what people say is generally seen as sufficient evidence of what they think" (p. 42).

Liebes and Katz (1990) used a focus group and interview technique with groups of people in their own homes to explore interpretations of *Dallas* from different cultural perspectives. They justified this choice of procedure by arguing that focus groups "were, in effect, operationalizing the assumption that small group discussions following the broadcast is a key to understanding the mediating process via which a program such as this enters the culture" (p. 28).

Liebes and Katz identified two kinds of interpretive talk in their interview transcripts: "referential discourse" (touching on life) and "critical discourse" (touching on art). To the extent that art represents life, whether accurately or not, these discourses cannot, of course, be entirely separated. As the critical-viewing skills agenda indicates, young children are seen as especially vulnerable to the deceptions of art, particularly where supposedly dangerous aspects of life such as violence or sexuality are concerned. Hence, children's ability to distinguish fantasy from reality in television and film has been the subject of much concerned investigation (Hawkins, 1977; Dorr, 1983; Nikken & Peeters, 1988; Potter, 1988; Dorr et al., 1990).

The extent to which the artistic features of art *help* children to formulate useful judgments about life—traditionally seen as one of the main functions of art—has been much less explored. Children as victims and dupes of art are a more common construct in research discourse about television than are children as connoisseurs, critics, and interpreters. As already mentioned in chapter 3, the case is very different when it comes to academic discussion of children's relationship with literature. A critic who powerfully draws attention to this inconsistency is John Hartley (1992) who argued, in an essay about television drama provocatively entitled "Photopoetics": "the two domains [of "high" literature and "low" television] are in much closer touch than [literary] rhetoric would suggest" (p. 153). Hartley argued against cultural relativism and lists a canon of television writers and producers who, he thinks, should be acknowledged as important creative talents. So, at a more populist level, did Bianculli (1992).

The relationship between the discourses of art and life, and how one informs judgments about the other, was the subject of my study, and the interview stage of the research was designed to get children talking about this relationship. However, talk data has special problems of research validity, particularly when children are involved.

THE SOCIAL CONTEXT OF TALK DATA

David Buckingham used interview and discussion techniques with schoolchildren in a number of studies, although he was fully aware of the problems of talk data. He pointed out that research methodology that seeks to use talk as its primary data needs to recognize the social context of the research situation, and to build this into the analysis. Much of his own research, therefore, used the naturalistic situation of the classroom to explore how groups of children negotiate interpretations of television in a social, rather than in an individualistic way. Buckingham argued that literacy, particularly the kind of literacy that comes from mass cultural products, cannot be defined as a set of skills belonging to individuals; it consists of socially determined and constructed meanings that are created through social interactions. Hence, for him, naturalistic research situations needed to be social ones, and the resultant talk needed to be analyzed as a group, rather than as an individual product. (Buckingham, 1993a).

My study also aimed to use talk to explore children's definitions of TV reality. The methodological problem was, as with Liebes and Katz's and Buckingham's studies, how to offer children the opportunity to make judgments about the realism or nonrealism of program elements, and to explain them in as naturalistic a way as possible, while providing reliable and recordable data. One way of doing this, as chosen by these earlier researchers, could have been a discussion group after the viewing event; bringing a group of children together in a naturalistic setting like a living room, or a classroom, and getting them talking in a systematic way about television material containing a variety of realistic and nonrealistic elements. However, such a technique, valuable though it can be in the examination of negotiations, relies on memory, which a long series of researchers, starting with Bartlett in the 1930s, has shown to be distorting (Bartlett, 1932). Such distortions are particularly common with narratives of events in which outside influences can profoundly alter memory for details of what happened. (Loftus & Palmer, 1974).

Talk data, relying on recall and divorced from the viewing situation to which it is referring, seemed unsuitable for the purpose of this research, which was to find out how children, in Liebes and Katz's (1990) words, "decoded what they see and hear," as a function of what exactly they were seeing and hearing (p. 20). The main focus of the study was to follow up Hodge and Tripp's (1986) investigations into children's awareness of modality, that is, the extent to which formal, aesthetic, and generic features of television material influenced judgments about what was real or not real. Such understandings, as Hodge and Tripp point out, are a form of literary judgment, and hence they are an essential component of any definition of literacy that includes critical, as well as basic decoding skills. Nor are they only aesthetic judgments. The view that young children cannot tell the difference between reality and fantasy in film and television is very widely held and has given rise to a number of educational initiatives designed to produce the trained viewer, who will be armed, or inoculated, against harmful effects.

In Brown's (1993) review of critical-viewing skills (or media literacy) programs in different countries, it was proposed that this training is especially necessary for elementary schoolchildren from kindergarten through grade 5 (the age group used in the present study). An implicit assumption of this proposal is that 5-to-11-year-old children do not yet have these skills and need to be taught them. The purpose of the present research was partly to test this assumption. Its other major aim was to discover specific instances of television artifice—or literary characteristics—that prompted children's judgments about reality and unreality, and to explore why. For this, an online measure was needed, a task that would enable observation of the children's response to an unreal situation on television as it occurred and which could follow up this response with some analysis of the children's reasoning.

PAUSING FOR COMMENT

The ability of viewers to comment on, and appreciate, the artifice of the TV medium—what Bianculli (1992) called tele-literacy—is increasingly recognized by program makers, leading to a kind of self-referentiality, which, if TV professionals were in the habit of using critical terminology, would be called postmodern. Postmodern art forms are "characterized by irony, pastiche and excess, they offer the pleasures of the 'popular' while simultaneously undermining the ideologies embedded in it by virtue of not taking them seriously" (Marshment, 1993, p. 144).

The experience of watching such self-referential programs requires viewers to experience a kind of Brechtian alienation, in which they are aware of the medium's artifice, but at the same time are enjoying the familiarity of the narratives. The process whereby program makers draw deliberate attention to their own production techniques, hence both celebrating and undermining them, was brought to a high level of dramatic sophistication in *Moonlighting* in the early 1980s, with the characters regularly addressing the camera and deconstructing the set by walking around it into another one, and, in the final episode, by doing it literally. Self-referentiality has since begun to appear regularly in the staple realistic settings of family sitcoms. In *Roseanne*, for instance, in the episode when a new actress playing Becky appeared, the whole cast commented on how annoying such character changes on TV were, and the studio audience roared with knowing laughter. The 1995 series of *Roseanne* abandoned all pretensions to realism; one episode had the whole cast playing *Gilligan's Island* (baffling to British viewers). Another brought Roseanne together with other sitcom mothers and initiated a discussion about how the roles of women in sitcom had changed from the 1950s onwards. Such subversions of the standard sitcom form are made possible by the producers' awareness that audiences have a long history of familiarity with this particular show, and also with the genre—they are, in Bianculli's phrase, tele-literate.

One of the most adventurous examples of this technique to be shown on prime-time television was a stimulus to the design of my study because it examined the meaning of reality and fantasy within a popular realistic television context. It was an episode of the family comedy *Growing Pains*, in which the character Ben, one of the teenage sons, dreamed he was a character in a family sitcom. The storyline required him to make a *Wizard of Oz*-like pilgrimage through the real TV studios, desperately trying to find his way back to real life, which, in this case, was actually his fantasy life. The other actors, all playing themselves, insisted on addressing him as Jeremy (the actor's real name), while he, in an increasing frenzy of identity crisis, kept insisting that he was Ben. It was very difficult even for the knowledgeable viewer to know who, of all the nonregular characters met by Ben/Jeremy in this nightmare, was an actor and who of the laughing bystanders was a genuine technician. Was the studio audience through which Jeremy/Ben stumbled in terror as he fled from the set, the real studio audience or a planted one? Was his terror real or acted? Given viewers' experience of entertainment programs like *Saturday Night Live,* in which the audience is often featured as a scripted part of the show, how real is a real studio audience anyway?

Eventually, the story had Ben waking from his nightmare and realizing that he was back in reality by looking around his bedroom (via a 180-degree point-of-view camera pan) and finding that it had a fourth wall. However, the final scene of the episode began playing with viewers' perceptions of reality once again. Ben turned on the television and saw his elder brother, Mike, trapped inside it begging to be let out and back into reality. With a cry of terror, Ben leapt over the sofa, and his leap was held in a freeze frame while the credits rolled; the question of what was real was left, literally, hanging in the air. Much of the humor of the episode sprang from the ironic way in which formal technical features were used to signal real and not real to Ben/Jeremy, and hence to the audience, as in the presence or absence of a fourth wall. The comic irony—quite a profound one—was that reality could only be seen through the eyes of the fictional character, Ben, not through the eyes of the real-life actor, Jeremy. Here, *Growing Pains,* like its model *The Wizard of Oz,* was making a fairly explicit claim for the power of art to show truths that everyday reality cannot show and, implicitly, for the sitcom form to be seen as art.

I watched this episode with my 12-year-old daughter, a *Growing Pains* fan, and it generated a great deal of discussion, which continues to this day (she is now 16). When I asked her what she thought of it, she said, "I thought it was really good," an aesthetic, not a moralistic judgment, referring to the quality of the writing and the performance. As such, it was very typical of young viewers' comments about programs (as appear later) and very untypical of much academic discourse about children and television, which concerns itself with the effects of unreality, not the pleasures of it. I thought the episode was good, too, and by another of the processes "via which a program such as this enters the culture," to quote Liebes and Katz (p. 28), the episode has become legendary in our family.

In cases like these, and many others, as Bianculli's book documented, producers invite collusion between themselves and viewers. There is a willingness on their part to hold up the action and say, "look how unreal this is (and isn't it enjoyable)." This not only requires a suspension of the suspension of disbelief, it also requires a high level of aesthetic appreciation. The play on reality and fantasy in this episode of *Growing Pains,* and its many allusions to other media products including *The Wizard of Oz* and the musical

Annie, as well as to its own "backstory," was an elaborate exercise in high comedy. It was meant to be seen as both clever and funny. Studies of children's metalinguistic ability, including the development of verbal humor and their understanding of irony in narratives (Dent & Rosenberg, 1990; Johnson & Pascual-Leone, 1989; Young, 1984) suggest that the doubly distancing process of suspending the suspension of disbelief should be beyond young children under the age of 7 or 8. Therefore, it might also be predicted that such young children would not be capable of any task that required them to hold up the action and comment on it. However, this is what popular television increasingly requires them to do, and this was what it was decided to ask them to do in the study.

COVIEWING AND DISCUSSION

An interview methodology was designed, using a coviewing setup, in which an adult interviewer introduced to the child as a friend or colleague of teacher or parent, sat and watched some videotaped television material alongside the child. The child was asked to hold the remote control and to pause the tape whenever they saw or heard something "that could not happen in real life". The child was then encouraged to discuss the reasons for his or her judgment. This had some artificial elements, notably the interviewing setup, and the presence of an audio tape recorder, but piloting showed that children were not particularly bothered by this. However, the procedure was naturalistic to the extent that it was modeled on the kind of situation that arises when viewers notice something implausible or something violating the normal conventions of television, as in the case of *Growing Pains*. There is plenty of anecdotal evidence that coviewing with children prompts extensive comment about art and life (e.g., Kinder, 1991), but it does not prompt much systematic research. However, ethnographic studies of children in their own homes, such as Palmer's (1986a, 1986b) show that they indulge in a great deal of comment, discussion, self-talk, monitoring, and what she calls "re-make" (using TV techniques in real-life play) while they watch television. There is nothing unnaturalistic about this kind of talk data.

RESEARCH ADVANTAGES

As a research technique, coviewing and on-the-spot discussion had a number of advantages: (a) It could identify exactly what sort of event or program characteristic strikes children as unreal; (b) Stopping the tape at this point would enable both interviewer and child to explore what was happening on the screen, at the time it happened; Thus, (c) the characteristic test-bias problem of young children not being able to describe verbally what they know (Murphy & Wood, 1983) is lessened: when the tape is paused, and the image frozen on screen, if the child finds it difficult to explain what he or she is referring to, the material is at hand to be examined. Furthermore, this technique did not rely on the vagaries of memory.

THE PILOT STUDY

The technique was piloted on six children between 4 and 11 years of age (who were not subjects in the main study) to test whether the task was manageable and had validity. It was important that the pilot children should see the point of what they were being asked to do and that they feel comfortable about doing it. All six of them cooperated well; they were not surprised by the task or tired by it, and between them they produced around 50 pages of interview transcripts.

As a result of piloting, it was clear that the term *real* required no elucidation for these children. They all understood exactly what was required—"something that couldn't really happen in real life." This was fortunate for the study's aim of keeping questions as open-ended as possible. There was no need to define for the children in the main study what was meant by real; it turned out to be a meaningful question even to the youngest children. Although there was no intention to use pre-schoolers in the study, two kindergarten-aged children volunteered for the pilot, and the opportunity was taken to find out how well they coped with it. Four-year-old Valda stopped the tape when she saw Big Bird and said, "Big Bird's not real." Asked why he was not real, she said: "I never saw him before."

> Interviewer: Did you ever see any of those children before? But are they real?
>
> Valda: Yeah
>
> Int: Why?
>
> Valda: Because they're people.
>
> Int: And what's Big Bird?
>
> Valda: He's a big yellow bird.

Unlike the older children used in the main study, Valda did not talk about Big Bird being a person dressed up. Her distinction between people and nonpeople as the basis for a reality judgment is characteristic of very young children's categorizations (Gardner, 1991). However, the preschool children talked much less freely than the older ones, and they lacked the vocabulary to provide the kind of critical discourse sought in the study; thus the decision not to use them seemed the right one.

Analysis of the pilot interview transcripts also generated a coding procedure for the main study interviews. The object of this analysis was, first, to identify what sort of televised events led to the pause button being pressed (for not real), and second, what sort of reasoning children of different ages would employ for making this judgment. The focus of analysis was on the children's modality references, that is, their use of formal, technical, aesthetic and generic features to identify what was or was not real. In analyzing these pilot transcripts, it became important to distinguish between the ability of children to identify what was not real, and their ability to explain why being unreal does not necessarily disqualify a program from being taken seriously. This distinction was seen as a fundamental aspect of a literate understanding of the relationship of art to life, a recognition, as Hodge and Tripp have argued, of the value of artifice, not of its dangers.

UNREAL BUT USEFUL

One of the pilot subjects, 11-year-old William, who produced ten pages of interview transcript, was particularly useful in establishing this distinction. William had had problems at school all his life, finding writing (though not reading) very difficult. However, as his mother somewhat resignedly explained, "he's a real expert on television." The authority and confidence with which he explained his reasoning was striking (talking about an animated sequence in *Sesame Street* in which flowers and houses and other everyday objects were depicted as triangular):

Interviewer: Why have you stopped the tape?

William: Stupid triangular cows.

Int: So?

William: Have you ever seen a triangular cow before? So–I don't think anybody has.

William was able to clarify the point that a perceived lack of reality per se does not mean that you should not "take a program seriously" (Dorr, 1983). Judgments about taking a program seriously also have to take into account the program's genre (a modality category) and the program's function for the audience (a pragmatic judgment, requiring knowledge of both producers' intentions and viewers' needs).

Int: You said that couldn't happen in real life about five times. Why do you think the producers do it that way?

William: It's just to teach the kids about the triangles and what the shapes are like, there are three corners, and three sides and stuff like that.

Int: So it doesn't matter if it's not real?

William: Not if it's a cartoon, like *Sesame Street*, but in real life it would be different.

Here, William points out the relevance of genre in assessing whether unreal elements in a program should disqualify it from having any educational value. For him, there is no problem in the case of *Sesame Street's* fake techniques: "It helps them [little kids] see the shape a lot and they remember it."

On the other hand, in a more realistic program like *The Cosby Show*, artificial elements such as the laughter track helped to alert William to the fact that "it's not a real family" and hence, can be taken less seriously:

They're just characters . . . like, when there's a real family and they make a crack, then nobody will laugh, because there's nobody like a massive audience out there watching them and going hahaha . . . but when you're in a TV show they have those big things up and they're told to applaud and they're in front of a big audience type of thing . . .

Interviewer: How do you know they're just characters?

William: Well, on the things that come up at the end, [meaning the credits] it says for Bill Cosby and the wife and everything, and there's different last names.

William's reference to the credits as a cue for knowing that the people in *The Cosby Show* were "just characters" was unique. None of our other interviewees mentioned titling, which for adult viewers is an obvious cue to reality status. It was an example of overlap between tele-literacy and the more conventional definition of the word—interestingly, in a child with a history of literacy problems.

TYPES OF MODALITY

As a result of piloting, a number of levels of reference were established. The first analysis of the transcripts identified the exact features that caused children to pause the tape. As in earlier studies, these features fell into two groups: reference to content aspects, such as story outcomes, and reference to formal features, such as special effects and production factors. These broadly corresponded to Liebes and Katz's art and life categories, and derived either from the children's own experience and their real-world knowledge, in the case of content/life references, or from their awareness of production processes, which obviously varied, in the case of form/art. Interestingly, some of the children's real-world knowledge such as how special effects like animation are created, came from television documentaries. It became clear that TV had provided useful opportunities for them to discuss how reality can be represented in nonreal ways—as with William's triangular cows being able to teach about shapes. The categories of events causing children to pause the tape, according to age group, are given in Figure 6.1. These are groupings of more detailed categories.

A further analysis of the transcripts as a whole, not just of the points at which children had paused the tape, revealed a number of subcategories of modality, 13 in all, used by the interviewees in their descriptions and explanations for TV events not being real (see Figure 5.1 on page 54). The first two columns, Impossible and Real/Improbable, refer to comments based on life rather than art (in Buckingham's terminology, external rather than internal explanations). The Impossible category (the largest group) includes all events that the children argued were impossible according to natural laws of physics and biology ("people can't fly"). The Real/Improbable category includes events that were unlikely forms of human behavior: "shopkeepers don't lend you money in real life." The other 11 categories listed in Figure 5.1 are references to different kinds of formal features of the TV material: special effects (the second largest group of references), narrative, genre, theater/performance, artistic/aesthetic features, and—a category that had to be included, as it is quite distinct, particularly for the youngest children—magic.

The third largest group of references, as Figure 5.1 showed, were Pragmatic. These were statements showing awareness of producers' intentions and effects on audiences, as with William's awareness that triangular cows made *Sesame Street* more appealing to its preschool audience. Within this category came pragmatic references to producer motivation, to institutional influences ('commercials are to make you buy things'), to design, planning, and to predicted impact on audiences. Many of these pragmatic judgments were combined with other kinds of references to production techniques. For example, in answer to the interviewer's question: "Why do you think the music is put there?" fifth grade Brad replied, "So it helps to know what's going to happen." There was also a small group of references, labeled Aesthetic, of which Brad's comment was an example, in which children showed awareness of artistic function or gave a direct response about how the program made them feel—good or scary. Brad's comment was labeled Pragmatic/Art.

As in this case, pragmatic statements were often allied to explanations about formal features, particularly in answer to the question, "Why is it done that way?" Such comments were given a separate combined coding: Pragmatic/Art, Pragmatic/Narrative, Pragmatic/Effects, and Pragmatic/Genre. This taxonomy of modality references is inevitably artificial and pulls apart some complex theorizing from the children about how formal techniques are utilized to create or not create impressions of reality. These definitions are discussed more fully in chapters 7–11.

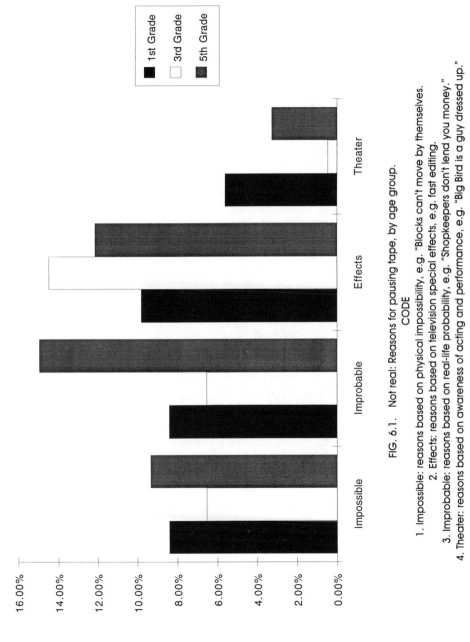

FIG. 6.1. Not real: Reasons for pausing tape, by age group.

1. Impossible: reasons based on physical impossibility, e.g. "Blocks can't move by themselves.
2. Effects: reasons based on television special effects, e.g. fast editing.
3. Improbable: reasons based on real-life probability, e.g. "Shopkeepers don't lend you money."
4. Theater: reasons based on awareness of acting and performance, e.g. "Big Bird is a guy dressed up."

THE SELECTION OF MATERIAL

Selecting material was subject to a number of constraints: In the first place, there was time: the pilot interviews demonstrated that about 10 to 15 minutes of tape, yielding between 30 and 50 minutes of conversation, was more than enough for the children's attention span and stamina. Hence, it was only possible to use short clips. There also had to be a reasonable range of genres to take account of children's experience of different TV material, and to allow for the inclusion of a variety of techniques and modality cues. Further, the material had to be suitable for children and to the teachers and parents whose permission was needed for the study. Hence, material with explicit violence was ruled out, despite the fact that much of the concern about children's reality judgments about TV centers around responses to violence. It was felt that deliberately showing violence to very young children as part of a research project could not be ethically justified. Nevertheless, the kinds of techniques used to represent dramatized violence on television and in film, such as suspense, fast editing, threat, music, verbal aggression, can also be found in other kinds of programming that is acceptable for children. It was children's awareness of the artifice of such techniques that interested us; such awareness, we hoped, could equally well be applied to interpretations of the representations of violence. This, indeed, is a fundamental assumption of critical-viewing-skills training. Under these constraints, four samples of programming were selected and edited for use in the pilot, and after the pilot one of the samples (from *Sesame Street*) was shortened to allow for the children's attention span, thus losing William's "stupid triangular cows."

Inevitably, the four samples of TV chosen did not represent a particularly normal television viewing experience. They were short (2 to 3 minute long) clips from: *Sesame Street* (a preschool educational program); *Real News for Kids* (a news program, preceded by commercials); *The Cosby Show* (a situation comedy); and *The Sand Fairy* (a fantasy period drama, based on *Five Children and It* by the Edwardian writer Edith Nesbit, produced by the BBC and shown on the Disney channel in the US). These included a wide variety of televisual formal techniques, ranging from animation in *Sesame Street* to canned laughter in *The Cosby Show.* There was also a variety of narratives and styles of address and of dramatic characterization. This choice of material was made on the basis of adult perceptions of variety, style, and technique, and on the basis of adult categorizations of genre. Of course, adult categorizations of TV material are not always the same as children's (Eke & Croll, 1992). Nevertheless, the same is true of programming provided in the TV schedules; it is adults who make the choices about what to show, and children have to make choices and responses within what is offered. Hence, this adult-directed selection seemed a valid procedure.

The interview procedure was open-ended: the questions were designed to elicit children's judgments of what seemed real or unreal features of television, and not to present them with predecided forced choices, as in Morison et al.'s 1981 study. There were no right or wrong judgments in this task, and it was expected that children would identify as unreal some features of the material that seemed quite realistic to an adult viewer. This proved to be the case; a striking example was the strong resistance by some interviewees to the idea that an older brother would let his little sister beat him at checkers, as realistically depicted in *The Cosby Show*. Third grader Paul, for example, "She couldn't beat somebody way older than her."

THE SEQUENCES

As already discussed, considerations of length (each sequence was between 2 and 3 minutes long); narrative coherence (each sequence had to be a self-contained scene or segment); genre (each sequence came from a different kind of programming); and a variety of uses of televisually stylistic, dramatic, narrative, and electronic techniques had to be included in the sample. The four sequences chosen according to these requirements, and the main events in the sequences, that caused the children to press the pause button for "couldn't happen in real life," with representative accounts of the children's responses, are described in the next chapters.

Although this program selection was clearly artificial, none of the pilot children made any objection to it, and neither did any of the children in the main study. Indeed, in the case of the drama programs, the fact that the sequences chosen were not complete gave rise to some intelligent and revealing speculation about the narrative and what might be happening, which would not otherwise have been elicited.

THE INTERVIEW SCHEDULE

As a result of the pilots, a simple interview schedule for the main study was drawn up. When the tape was stopped by the child, follow-up prompt questions were asked. The first was: Why couldn't that happen in real life? to explore the child's reasoning for identifying nonreality. Second, the children were asked: How do you think that was done? to explore their metaknowledge of the medium's techniques. Third, they were asked: Why do you think it's done that way? to explore their pragmatic awareness of intent. Where the children referred to "they," they were asked who "they" were, again to explore pragmatic awareness. At the end of each TV sequence the child was asked: What kind of program was that? and How was it different from the one we just saw? to explore their knowledge of genre. Finally, they were asked about audience awareness: What sort of people would watch it? and for their own critical opinion:

Do you think it's a good program? Why? Why not? These final questions at the end of each sequence were only asked if the information had not already been volunteered in the course of the child's comments. They were only asked, too, if the children were still happy to keep talking. Where they seemed tired or eager to go off to their next class, they were not asked. The interviews were carried out by a male and female interviewer, both previously introduced to the children, with the supervision of the class teacher who was teaching in an adjacent room. The interviewers alternated between boy and girl interviewees.

The pilot interviews suggested that the technique was something that could be understood and operated by children within the target age groups, that it was capable of eliciting discriminating information about how children made judgments about the believability or nonbelievability, of television material, and why this was. However, it was time consuming, not only because of the time needed for interviews, but also because of the need for transcription; hence it could only be used on a comparatively small number of children (18).

EXPLAINING THE RESEARCH: CULTURAL DOPES?

In line with the underlying premise of the research that child audiences—whether for researchers, or for television—are not, to use James Anderson's (1990) resonant phrase, "cultural dopes," it was decided to be completely honest with the children in the study about why the research was being carried out. It was explained to them that we were interested in finding out what children thought about television, especially what was real and unreal, because it was a question many grown-ups were concerned about and talked about. However, children's views on television were not usually heard, and that was why we wanted to talk to them. Adult disapproval of television, and the lack of opportunity to talk about it were issues these children could understand; television was not favored in their schools, being seen as somewhat inimical to reading.

PREDICTIONS

In line with developmental accounts of metalinguistic development such as Young's (1984), the more complex, pragmatic level of modality reference, involving inference and attribution, should be more frequent in older children. However, as Buckingham (1988) pointed out, higher levels of processing from a print-literacy perspective may not apply to the processing of television material, which requires children to follow complex narratives and to make pragmatic attributions about characters and events from a very early age—often well before they are able to decode "lower" units of meaning, such as single printed words. Hence, it was quite possible that no age differences would be found in these kinds of pragmatic references, and so it proved, in some individual cases.

It was also predicted, in line with Dorr's and her colleagues' research (Dorr, 1983; Dorr et al., 1990), that purely physical televisual features would be more salient for younger children as a benchmark of reality/non-reality, whereas older children would be more likely to take televisual special effects as given, and would focus on unlikely or improbable real-world human behavior. Of course, all these judgments would be a function of the kinds of material to be shown to the interview subjects. This was the main area of inquiry of the study: How would children's knowledge of life influence their judgments about art and vice versa?

7

"A Show for Little Kids": Sesame Street

Bearing in mind the constraints described in chapter 6, sequences from four TV programs were chosen for use in the study. This chapter and the next three examine the four sequences and the events in them that the children deemed not to be possible in real life. As described, the children's task was to press the pause button on the video remote control whenever they saw or heard something in these four sequences that they thought could not happen in real life. The pilot interviews had demonstrated that this was a feasible task for children in the age groups concerned, and that it yielded a variety of conversational responses that could be usefully analyzed for modality references and critical reasoning. All these conversations, including the interviewers' questions, the children's responses, and the soundtrack of the programs, were recorded on audio tape. The transcripts of these conversations formed the data for the following analyses. Sample transcripts are given in full in the appendices on pp. 185–226.

The transcripts were analyzed in two ways: First, a note was made of every point at which the children stopped the tape. This yielded a breakdown of the events in each program most likely to be chosen as "couldn't happen in real life" by several children, and events that were only chosen by one or two. These breakdowns are shown in graph form in Figure 6.1 on page 77. There were 81 pauses altogether for *Sesame Street*, 47 for *Real News for Kids*, seven for the commercials, 19 for *The Cosby Show*, and 68 for *The Sand Fairy*—222 pauses altogether spread across 69 different "unreal" events.

The second analysis of the transcripts categorized the modality references. These came not just from the children's initial comments when they paused the tape, but from the whole series of conversational ex-

82

changes between each child and the interviewer. These conversational exchanges were follow-up elaborations on the initial comments, in some cases quite extensive, in others very brief. Modality references were analyzed according to the groupings derived from the pilot interviews, as shown in Figure 5.1, page 54.

PAUSING FOR COMMENT: SESAME STREET

Sesame Street is the most universally watched educational preschool children's program in the world. It penetrates into around 98% of its target audience's homes in the United States, including its particular audience, the economically deprived (Palmer, 1988), and it is now seen in some form in 30 different countries (Gettas, 1992). During its 26 years of broadcasting on public television in the United States, its Muppet characters have become instantly recognizable, and although the program has aroused controversy over its commercially based production styles, and lately from right wing Republicans over the fact that it is publicly funded, it continues to be popular and to attract federal funding (Davies, 1995). All the children used in the study were familiar with it.

The *Sesame Street* sequence included three segments, each one utilizing different forms characteristic of the program's style. First, there was a short (45 second) drawn animation sequence about the letter T, showing a cartoon pirate digging for buried treasure on a desert island. The island was represented in the conventional, newspaper-cartoon style of a small, sandy knoll with a palm tree on it. Again conventionally, the pirate wore ragged clothes, and there was a sailing ship in the background in the first shot. The pirate identified where the treasure was buried by noticing a large T in the sand. He dug furiously and rapidly until he found a wooden chest full of golden Ts. On the soundtrack there was portentous trumpet music, and a voice saying, "The letter T." Then came another animation segment, this time a stop-frame film sequence of toy blocks moving by themselves and forming themselves into a cat, which was then knocked down by a real cat. This was accompanied by jaunty electronic organ music. In contrast to the drawn animation sequence, where the fact of the animation itself was not identified as unreal by anybody, this use of stop-frame animation was universally seen as not real; it was one of only two techniques to cause the pause button to be pressed by all the children. (The other unanimous vote came in *The Sand Fairy*.)

The final *Sesame Street* sequence was a sketch set in a studio living room with a real person, the male presenter (Bob) teaching Big Bird, who, as one child put it, is "a guy in a costume," to play the piano loudly and softly. As well as being an introduction to the concepts of loud and soft, (a standard *Sesame Street* pedagogic strategy), the sequence was also a comic lesson in patience, another favorite *Sesame Street* technique—recognition humor for parents of demanding and persistent toddlers who are likely to be watching the show. During the lesson, Bob was constantly interrupted by Big Bird with requests for explanation and with complaints about being too hot or too cold (more concepts), and requests for Bob to open or shut the window (yet more concepts). Further interruptions came from phone calls, from noises outside the window, and finally from a knock at the door from Gordon, Bob's fellow presenter, who was returning a borrowed magazine and looked very surprised at having Bob snatch the magazine, and slam the door in his face. The program is designed to appeal to both adults and children (Lovelace, Scheiner, Dollberg, Segui, & Black, 1994); however, this adult dimension was not mentioned by any of our child respondents. Nobody, for instance, thought that Big Bird was being unrealistically demanding. The children all watched it with completely straight faces. College students, on the other hand, to whom I have shown the program as a demonstration of prosocial uses of television, have usually found the sequence hilarious, because they can take an adult perspective while recognizing their own former childish behavior.

Thus, the *Sesame Street* clip (brief though it was) covered a great deal of stylistic and conceptual ground (as the program itself does), and it included a variety of presentational techniques, including a brief educational narrative (the T treasure story); a simple demonstration of stop-frame animation with no particular narrative or conceptual underpinning; and a realistic comic narrative showing a very recognizable human situation in which, however, human beings and a large yellow Muppet were integrated without comment. It was expected that both the stylistic techniques and the behavior of the characters would prompt the pressing of the pause button. It was also possible that the rapid editing and complete discontinuities of the subject matter might prompt some children to say that it was unreal to cut from a shot of a cartoon pirate to one of a pile of blocks. This would be more likely with viewers not familiar with the show or with American commercial television, which was not the case with these children—another example of developing tele-literacy. (However, rapid intercutting from one person and setting to another was later identified as unreal by a number of children in a sequence in *Real News for Kids*—see p. 98.)

PAUSING FOR COMMENT

Twelve different events in *Sesame Street* prompted children to press the pause button for not real. Five were chosen by only one child each. Three events produced almost unanimous responses across the three age groups. These were the use of the letter T in the treasure island cartoon sequence the blocks moving by themselves and Big Bird. Table 7.1 gives a breakdown of these events.

"THAT ISN'T A REAL TREASURE: THAT'S A T"

None of the interviewees had any problems in understanding the task: to press the pause button whenever they saw or heard something that could not happen in real life. Accordingly, the tape of the selected segments had hardly started when the first event occurred to be identified as not real, and it was identified by nearly all the children. Fourteen of the 18 pressed the pause button when they saw the letter T as a sign on the ground, indicating the whereabouts of a buried chest of golden letter Ts. None of the children, not even the most technology-wise fifth graders, referred to the animation itself as being not real.

The 14 who pressed for the letter T included all six first graders (6- and 7-year-olds). Four of them gave as their reason that treasures did not usually consist of Ts; their reasoning was drawn from knowledge of life as distinct from art, and was hence classified as an Improbable judgment. However, artistic considerations soon came in, illustrating how complex modality judgments can be, and how formal and structural considerations cannot be separated from judgments about content:

Joe (first grade): That wasn't true because gold can't be a T.

Jack (first grade): There couldn't be T treasures.

Natasha (first grade): They really wouldn't have a T for a treasure.

TABLE 7.1
Number of Times Events Were Identified as "Not Real" in *Sesame Street*: All Children (Base 18, 6 in Each Age Group)

Sesame St.	All 4/5	All 3rd	All 1st	All Children	Boys	Girls
TV Event						
Letter T	4	4	6	14	9	5
Blocks	6	8	13	27	16	11
Big Bird	6	2	5	13	6	7
Voice on phone	3	0	3	6	4	2
Coincidence	7	2	1	10	7	3
Fast digging	2	0	1	3	3	0
Cat not real	1	0	0	1	1	0
No pirates	1	0	0	1	1	0
Jumping	1	0	0	1	1	0
No treasure	0	0	3	3	1	2
False jewels	0	1	0	1	0	1
Not real pirate	1	0	0	1	1	0
Total	32	17	32	81	50	31

This reasoning was drawn from their real-world knowledge about the usual likely form of treasures—coins or jewels. Similar commonsense judgments were applied to the painting of the T on the ground, to which four children objected, for example:

> Anna: People don't paint Ts on the ground.

More complex objections were offered by a few of the children. One first-grade boy drew on narrative and generic expectations to object to the use of the letter T to "mark the spot":

> Int: Why have you pressed?
>
> Philip: Because it's usually an 'X'.
>
> Int: It's usually an X for what?
>
> Philip: For where gold is.

Philip's objection to the T—and his pressing of the pause button to indicate that it was not real—came not just from general knowledge about buried treasure, but from his knowledge of stories about buried treasures and their usual conventions. This may have been in the other first-graders' minds too, but they did not make it explicit. This specifically literary objection was also made by two third graders and two fourth/fifth graders. Lauren (fourth grade) not only drew on her knowledge of the generic conventions of treasure-island stories, but also on her experience of the teaching methods of *Sesame Street*:

> Lauren: There really couldn't be a big T on the ground.
>
> Int: Why not?
>
> Lauren: Because a lot of times X marks the spot, and they're teaching kids a different letter.

The greater frequency of such metajudgments among older children, drawing on their knowledge of what normally happens in art as well as what happens in life, was as expected. Further discussion with the younger children would possibly have drawn out more complex judgments from them, too, and in a classroom situation, teachers could explore such metajudgments further. What emerged clearly with Philip and Lauren's responses (and it was not predicted from previous research) was the use of artistic criteria as a standard for reality or unreality; The T was not real, not because Ts do not usually appear in the sand in real life, but because it violated the normal conventions of stories about buried treasure. This appears to add a further dimension of reality judgment to the taxonomies already produced by Hawkins (1977) and Potter (1988).

"BLOCKS DON'T MOVE BY THEMSELVES"

The next event to produce a generally agreed judgment of nonreality was the stop-frame sequence of toy blocks moving by themselves to form a model of a cat. This was one of only two events in the four different clips that produced pauses from every single child (the other was the floating baby in *The Sand Fairy*). It also produced the most number of pauses; a number of the youngest children pressed the button every time the blocks moved.

The responses to the blocks moving fell into two categories. One category consisted of explanations of why blocks could not move, the other category consisted of explanations of how the animation was done. The children who explained why blocks moving by themselves could not be real made reference to the laws of physics and biology:

> Anna, (first grade), Amy, (first grade), Sarah, (fourth grade): They are not alive.

> Paul (third grade): Blocks don't have brains.

> Ruth. (third grade): They have no legs to get up and walk.

All interviewees were asked how they thought the animation was done: two first graders, two third graders, and three fourth/fifth graders suggested that it was done with "invisible string." One third grade boy and one fifth grade boy suggested that it was magnetic:

> Ryan (third grade): They must have had a magnet under it to make it move

A fifth grade boy, and a fourth grade girl gave clear, accurate explanations of stop-frame animation:

> Int: How do you think that is done?

> Brad: With clay animation. They move it a little bit and they take a shot of that and they move it again and take another shot.

> Lauren: First they stop the film and they move it and they stop it and they fix it and they start the film again.

> Int.: Have you done something like this?

> Lauren: No.

> Int: But you know how it is done. How do you know?

> Lauren: Because I watched some stuff on special effects.

One fifth grade boy who was exceptionally knowledgeable about television and computer effects, produced an odd combination of the primitive string idea and technical knowledge:

Ben: Blocks can't move themselves. They're moving it with fishing line, I would guess. Or they would, what they would do is they would do just like I'm doing, like, take the block like that. [*Moving a book on a table*]. Okay? Shoot one—24 frames in a second—then stop it, move, stop, move, stop, move.

First graders found it almost impossible to produce a coherent explanation of this technique although some struggled valiantly to express the ideas they clearly had:

Joe: They like put—I think it's a little hole but you can't see it, it's all around, and they get a little thing on the ground and move it around, or . . .

Although none of the children fully articulated the fact that stop-frame animation is unreal because it makes real objects do things they cannot normally do, it would seem that, to these children, this kind of animation more obviously violates the natural laws of real world behavior than the cartoon kind (as used in the pirate sketch). One or two children made reference to the very fast digging of the pirate in the cartoon segment, for instance:

Philip (first grade): Oh, they can't dig that fast; they get like down there in two seconds.

Int: How can they make it look so fast?

Philip: Fast-forwarding.

But generally, the blatantly artificial conventions of drawn cartoons appeared to be accepted on their own terms by this group of children, whereas the use of special techniques—strings, magnets, stopping and starting the camera—to manipulate real-world objects was not accepted as real. For these children, art had its own standards that could be accepted as normal, conventional, and real in some cases (as with drawn cartoons), but not in others (as with stop-frame animation). The other difference between the two sequences was generic: the cartoon pirate sequence was a narrative, a form with which children were familiar, whereas the blocks sequence was not; it was simply a demonstration of the technique and as such rather puzzling.

"IT'S JUST A GUY IN A COSTUME": BIG BIRD

The next most frequently-identified not-real feature of *Sesame Street* was Big Bird. Five first graders, two third graders, and all six fourth/fifth graders pressed the pause button when they first saw Big Bird (sitting on a piano stool next to Bob). The two first grade boys who pressed pause gave idiosyncratic reasons for Big Bird not being real, for instance, 6-year-old Philip:

Int: Why did you press?

Philip: Because Big Bird is so fat! He can't sit on that bench with him, too, if it's a real piano bench.

Int: So why is that not like real life?

Philip: They probably have a bigger bench - like a piano bench - but he can't fit on it because he's too big.

And Jack: People don't let birds in their house.

In contrast, all three first grade girls gave modality-theater reasons for Big Bird's nonreality, drawing on their knowledge of costume, acting, and dressing up, as well as their knowledge about the program. For instance:

Anna: It is really a person, and the neck is part of the costume.

These girls, too, referred to real-world knowledge about birds.

Amy: Birds can't talk and they can't be so big.

The size of Big Bird was also picked up as a modality cue by the three third graders who talked about him (of whom only two pressed the pause button). As Elijah (10) put it, "He couldn't be real because he is too big of a bird." Again, it was the two girls, not the boy, who used theatrical references to explain why Big Bird was not real: "He was in a costume, he couldn't be real" (Ruth, 10) and, "I think it is a man in a suit, or a woman in a suit, playing the piano" (Louise, 9).

All six fourth/fifth graders pressed the button for Big Bird. As Tim (11) put it succinctly: "He is fake. . . . He is just a costume or somebody's in it." Eve also used the costume as her reason for identifying Big Bird's unreality. Surprisingly, two of these older children did not make reference to the blatant theatricality of Big Bird, but referred to the real-world fact that real birds do not talk. These two girls (Lauren and Sarah) in other respects used very sophisticated reasoning based on literary and stylistic features, but in this case, did not refer to the pretty obvious fact that Big Bird was an actor in a costume. Although they are only a very small sample, this finding is consistent with the lack of interest in technical effects shown by older girls in their questionnaire answers about "how the pictures change on TV," in contrast to younger girls and particularly, to older boys.

The two most articulate fifth grade boys in the interview group went over the top in the other direction, offering highly technical explanations for the way Big Bird was "done":

Brad: Big Bird is not real.

Int: What is Big Bird if he is not real?

Brad: I'm not really sure about that. I don't know whether he is a robot because they have a voice for a robot.

Ben: Big Bird isn't real. . . I know how they do that.

Int: How?

Ben: Well, let's see. You would have two men to control a puppet like that. Okay. There's a man in here that controls the body movements from the neck down. The head is a robot . . . You look up, you see like that, okay? It's kind of like a mechanical periscope. Like, look at it and it goes out little holes in his eyes, and to control the mouth movements, there's a guy behind the cameraman. He uses a little joystick. It takes a lot of work to get it just right. He uses that and there's a microphone that he has. So it's kind of like a ventriloquist. You have to talk into the microphone and do the mouth movements in really good time at the same time.

Ben was an exceptional interviewee because he had a great deal of technical knowledge. Nevertheless, this knowledge did not necessarily make him literate. It was his understanding of why a "fake" big bird was useful in *Sesame Street* that best demonstrated his level of understanding:

Int: So what's the point of Big Bird?

Ben: Well, just for kids, that they might believe that he's real . . . He teaches kids about triangles and like lessons, you know.

Int: Why a bird rather than a person?

Ben: Well, kids can adapt to that better. Like, um, they listen to *people* all the time, and it's just nicer if it's animals like that doing it.

This pragmatic audience awareness was also found in younger respondents: For instance, Anna (first grade), in answer to the same question about why Big Bird was used in the program, answered, "To help them [kids] to learn. There are usually number things and alphabet things and some other things." And third-grade Elijah stressed a key aspect of the character's and the program's appeal: "[They do it that way] so it's more fun to watch."

"THAT COULDN'T HAPPEN . . . THAT THE DOOR BELL AND THE TELEPHONE WOULD RING."

As Table 7.1 shows, nearly all the other *Sesame Street* responses were made by only one or two children to specific aspects of the three events already mentioned, with the exception of one event: The Coincidence.

This was not a technically unrealistic aspect of the program, and the fact that it was picked up so often as "not likely to happen in real life" was one of the first surprises of the children's responses. Clearly, it was a judgment drawn from real life (Improbable), and the children were emphatic in their objections to it. It was picked up by five of the oldest group (two of them twice), two of the third graders, and one of the first graders. In the sketch, each time Bob began to play the piano, the phone would ring, or Big Bird would interrupt, or there would be a knock at the door or window. Joe (first grade) gave a fair summary of the general objections:

> Joe: (pressing pause): As soon as he touched it [the piano], it went ring (giving a ringing sound.)
>
> Int: Why couldn't that happen?
>
> Joe: Because the phone, because, it's not really possible 'cos it takes a lot of time until somebody calls you when you're playing the piano, 'cos as soon as you touch it—so it's not real.

Then, the next time Bob was interrupted:

> Int: Why have you pressed pause?
>
> Joe: Because as soon as he plays the piano something happens.
>
> Int: And why is that not like real life?
>
> Joe: Because it, because if it does it once, it can't do it twice and then a third time and then another time.

All of the children who pressed pause for this series of coincidences referred either to the timing and the frequency of the interruptions, like Joe, or to their own experiences. For instance, Tim (fifth grade): "I play the piano, and nothing ever happens." Sarah (fourth grade) and Ben (fifth grade) knew the right word:

> Sarah: That kind of thing could happen, but really it wouldn't. It could be a coincidence.
>
> Ben: There wouldn't be that much of a coincidence, I don't think.

Generally, the children were baffled as to why the sequence had been set up with all these interruptions, and could not see the point of it. Lauren (fourth grade) volunteered that it could be 'to teach people the different sounds.' Ben, again showing his unusual sophistication, identified the humor of the event and its narrative function:

> Ben: It's supposed to be kind of funny. Distractions—like, there wouldn't be a point to the story if he taught him the piano by hearing like that.

As Table 7.1 shows, all the other incidents of children pressing the pause button were associated with these four events. The voice on the phone, identified as not real on six occasions, was an electronic squeaky voice—one of the interruptions to the piano lessons. The other events, picked up by only one or two children, were details of the treasure sequence ("they are not real jewels; there's no such thing as treasure; they are not real pirates"). Ben (fifth grade) also argued that the cat in the stop-frame sequence was not real—and in fact, it was.

In summary, the children identified a variety of technical and theatrical effects in *Sesame Street* ("fast forwarding"; sound effects; stop frame animation; dressing up in a bird costume) as "not real", and their reasons were generally drawn from real-world knowledge about the normal behavior of blocks, birds, and human beings. Underlying these reasons—and made explicit by a few articulate children—were objections to violations of artistic, rather than real-world, conventions, as in the use of a T instead of an X "to mark the spot". In the case of the coincidental interruptions to the piano lesson, children drew on their own experience; they knew that it was unlikely for domestic activities to be interrupted with such regularity. Again, the more literate children—usually the oldest ones—were able to articulate why this was happening: for humorous and narrative effect. Younger children were much more likely than older ones to give idiosyncratic responses and reasoning, many of which, however, were evidence of imaginative thinking and, hence, were literate, if not accurate, responses. These responses illustrate that the critical-viewing-skills approach, which seeks to demystify the techniques of television, is not the same thing as encouraging literacy. Philip's (first grade) comment that Big Bird was unrealistic because he was too fat to sit on the piano stool (rather than because he was "a guy in a costume") represented intelligent and literate observation and reasoning at his own level. This was more relevant to him than a desire to deconstruct aspects of perform-ance and costume would have been. Such deconstructive analyses come later in childhood.

8

"Everyone is Talking About Ross Perot": Real News for Kids

The next item on the tape was "real," a clip from *Real News for Kids*, the Fox Channel's laudable attempt to provide hip-style news in which children aged between eight and 14 would be interested. The choice of title was interesting from the point of view of this study, seeming to imply that there is such a thing as unreal news for kids. Given the production values and obvious efforts made with the program, the title could certainly be read as making a strong claim to legitimacy and quality, in contrast to much of the programming offered to children in the United States which is cheap animation.

The clip from *Real News for Kids* was preceded by commercials for a drawing toy, The Imagineer, and for Swanns Crossing dolls (Barbie and Ken-type models based on characters from a now-defunct soap opera). The drawing-toy ad used speeded-up film to show drawings magically materializing; the doll ad had girl models, aged 10 or 11, discussing the behavior of the characters and moving them around with stilted and stereotyped conversations about clothes and dating—an aspect that, although it antagonized every adult who saw it, was not identified as unrealistic by a single child, male or female, in the study. Then the news program opened with a montage of special effects: a graphics title sequence showing revolving heads through which goldfish and other images appeared to be swimming, backed by a series of rapidly changing images including a revolving globe to represent the changing days of the week. There was insistent brassy music on the soundtrack, as with adult-news bulletins.

The news sequence used in the study had two segments: first, three brief previews from reporters about what they were going to be reporting on: a scene in an ice rink to introduce an item about the film *The Mighty*

Ducks; then, a sequence about Ross Perot dropping out and then dropping back in to the Presidential election campaign; and finally, an introduction to an item about the Vietnam War memorial wall in Washington. The Ross Perot preview consisted of several different talking heads edited to follow each other in quick succession, all saying the words "Ross Perot".

Following these teasers was a full news item about the U.S. economy, in which the presenter explained the national debt in terms of a shopper rushing round a toy store and buying everything whose appearance he liked. This sequence, with the presenter's voice-over describing what he was doing, used speeded-up motion and was obviously staged. The shopper ended up having to borrow money from the store keeper to pay for everything he had bought. At the end of the shopping trip, he discovered the error of his ways, when he owed the storekeeper so much with interest that he did not have enough money to buy a much-desired ticket for a baseball game. This elaborate kid-in-a-toy-store metaphor, obviously designed to have particular relevance for children, produced some interesting misreadings, which are described later.

The events identified as not real in these linked sequences are itemized in Tables 8.1 & 8.2.

"COMMERCIALS ARE FAKE"

Only three children—all boys—pressed pause for events that "couldn't happen in real life" in the commercials: the ever-vigilant Ben (fifth grade), Tim (fifth grade), and first-grade Philip. Ben took the opportunity to give another complex explanation of the persuasive techniques of commercials (see p. 138); Philip identified the speeded-up drawing (a special electronic effect—art) and the plastic skirts of the dolls (as distinct from real clothes—a life reference) as unreal. Most of the children did not see fit to comment on the techniques used in the commercials. It is unlikely,

TABLE 8.1
Number of Times Events Identified as Not Real in Commercials
Before Real News for Kids (All children: Base 18, 6 in Each Age Group)

Commercials	All 4/5	All 3rd	All 1st	All Children	Boys	Girls
All comercials are fake	1	0	0	1	1	0
Paper in Imagineer toy	1	0	0	1	1	0
Sets in Swanns Crossing toy	1	0	0	1	1	0
No dolls on tv	1	0	0	1	1	0
Fast drawing	0	0	1	1	1	0
Not real skirts	0	0	1	1	1	0
TOTAL	4	0	2	6	6	0

TABLE 8.2
Number of Times Events Identified as Not Real in *Real News for Kids*:
All Children (Base 18)

Real News	*All 4/5*	*All 3rd*	*All 1st*	*All Children*
$20 not enough	1	2	1	4
Ross Perot	3	1	1	5
Animation	1	1	2	4
Toys not liked	1	0	0	1
Couldn't buy stuff in time	1	0	1	2
Store keeper wouldn't lend money	4	1	2	7
Audio in voice	1	0	1	2
Heads in credits	2	4	2	8
Fast movement	2	3	1	6
Camera wouldn't be in Washington D.C.	0	1	0	1
Camera wouldn't be at rink	0	1	0	1
Heads under water (credits)	0	1	0	1
Fake money	0	1	0	1
Wouldn't say 'eeny' to the president	0	0	1	1
The way people are dressed	0	0	1	1
Not him on Thursdays	0	0	1	1
Total	16	17	14	47

however, that they did not notice their artifice. Given the children's general awareness of commercial techniques, as evidenced in their questionnaire answers, it is more likely that, along with much of the adult population, these children see commercials as generally operating in the realm of the unreal, or at least the hyperbolic, and they probably saw little point in saying so over and over again. As Tim put it, "I think all commercials are fake . . . they are just for advertising."

DECONSTRUCTING THE NEWS

There is a marked difference in the spread of incidents identified as unreal in the *Real News* item compared with the *Sesame Street* item, where most of the pauses were associated with a fairly high degree of consensus. Most of the pauses in *Real News* (as Table 8.2 shows) belong only to one or two children each. Although the item was about the same length as the *Sesame Street* segments, and despite the use of a variety of special effects, the *Real News* item and its preceding commercials produced only half as many pauses as the *Sesame Street* item. This suggests that an item labeled "News," featuring events and people that children know from other sources, belong in real life and should be "taken seriously," as Dorr put it. Hence, allowances seem to have been made for quite blatant violations of reality, such as the speeded-up motion with background music in the shopping sequence, perhaps because the activity itself was real. Only six children—two in first grade, two in fourth/fifth, and three in third grade—pressed pause for this, although all must have noticed it.

Similarly, the title sequence showing revolving heads with floating graphics superimposed on them produced the highest number of pauses (8) in the *Real News* sequence, in contrast to the unanimous vote of 18 for the moving blocks in *Sesame Street*. The graphics were obviously a manipulation of reality, but because title sequences often present unlikely looking montages of images, it seems probable that many children were aware of this and did not think the sequence worth commenting on; fancy-looking titles obey the rules of art, not of life. As Sarah, (fourth grade) put it, "It is not supposed to be real. It's just the beginning of the thing and they usually do things like that."

Third graders commented most often on the unreality of the titles. As Ryan put it: "I don't think he can really have things go through his head." First-grade Jack also pointed out how impossible the events were, "People can't fly sideways and they can't go up and swash their heads." But having "a.b.c.s floating through their heads" as third grade Louise put it, was perceived by older children to have a legitimate communication function:

Int: Why do you think they have done it this way?

Louise: To make it look appealing and crazy and interesting. . .

Ruth (fourth grade) agreed: To make it look funny . . . so kids would watch it.

Where animation was used in the news titles, four children (two first, one third and one fifth grader) identified it as unreal. In contrast, no children had found the cartoon animation in *Sesame Street* unreal. Although it is important to be cautious about drawing general conclusions from such a small, unrepresentative sample, there does seem to be some evidence from this group of children of different rules of reality judgment being applied to different genres. Although animation is okay in a preschool program, it may be less so in a news program intended for older children.

"THEY WANT TO GIVE YOU THE FEELING THAT EVERYBODY IS TALKING ABOUT ROSS PEROT"

Most of the incidents identified as not real in the *Real News* sequence were associated with special effects, and were identified as having merely an attention-getting function ("appealing," "funny," etc.) However, the item included one striking use of special effects that was intrinsically related to an underlying conceptual idea. This was the use of rapid intercutting between several shots of different public figures, including the then Democratic presidential candidate, Bill Clinton, and the then President George Bush, with each person saying just two words: "Ross Perot." One child—third-grade Louise—articulated the point of this: "It's to give you the feeling that everybody is talking about Ross Perot."

Five children—three fourth/fifth graders, two third graders and one first grader—pressed the pause button when they saw this sequence, and all their reasons for saying that it could not happen in real life were variants on the realization that it would not be possible to get all these people together at once, and, therefore, some form of editing must have been used although nobody (not even Ben) used the word *montage*. Lauren's (fourth grade) comments are typical of the older children's reasoning:

> Lauren: They had different people from all over and that couldn't really be in one TV studio. You would have to film it from all different places.
>
> Int: What is the point of doing that?
>
> Lauren: To tell you all the different views and what everyone is talking about. You don't have to wait with just one, and you can get people from all over the world and tape them and bring them back to where you're shooting the actual video.

First-grade Philip expressed a similar idea, but in his own terms. Having pointed out that viewers are not really "taken round the world" by reporters, as the presenter promised, he gave his own version of how global news roundups were done:

> Philip: They get someone on one flight and then they take him over Africa and someone's on America and then there's someone over Mexico and then they take the kid across America off the [unclear] and put him on Mexico and then someone gets like, to Australia or Mexico, and they take the Mexican guy off and say here we are in Mexico, and like that.

The children who identified this rapid intercutting as not real clearly had some conception of editing, although none used the word, and the younger children, like Philip, had their own rather endearing idiosyncratic theories about the process. Louise's (third grade) account was the most succinct:

> Louise: They probably got a tape that said 'Ross Perot' on the tape and they probably got another person that said 'Ross Perot' and I think they put the tapes on at the same time.

Further awareness of editing was shown in responses to *The Sand Fairy* (see chapter 10) and also in the questionnaire data (see chapter 5).

"YOU CANNOT BUY ALL OF THAT WITH ONLY TWENTY DOLLARS"

All the aforementioned incidents referred to art, that is, it was technical aspects of the program that caused children to press the pause button for unreal. However, there was one representation of behavior that was judged by knowledge of life rather than of art, and produced a degree of consensus about the unreality of the news item, particularly among the older children: this centered around the economics of the shopping sequence. In this item, the presenter rushed around a toy store—his speed exaggerated by "fast forwarding" as Philip put it—buying as many toys as he could, having borrowed $20 from the store keeper. Ruth (third grade) thought that the money was fake. She then pointed out, "You cannot buy all of that with only twenty dollars," a point also made by Philip (first grade). One first grader, Natasha, found the incident unrealistic for a different reason: "You can't buy that many toys because they would be hard to carry."

The other related unreal aspect of this incident was the storekeeper lending money to the over-spending shopper. As with an incident in *The Cosby Show* where Theo allowed his little sister Rudy to beat him at checkers, such altruistic behavior was viewed with deep suspicion by a number of interviewees, and, in this case, girls were more suspicious than boys:

> Eve (fourth grade): The store keeper gave him money . . . that probably wouldn't happen.

> Lauren (fourth grade): No store manager would give someone money.

> Sarah (fourth grade): A store person wouldn't lend a person money.

> Anna (first grade): People don't usually give other people money.

Although they found the incident unbelievable, one or two of the children grasped the point of the analogy, although most did not, or at least could not express it. Ben (fifth grade) put it most clearly: "They're doing it [this way] for the story—to explain how the government is spending like a kid in the toy store." Despite this sophisticated understanding, Ben still viewed the item with a childlike literalness, being particularly indignant about the shoddy quality of the toys being bought:

> Ben: His friends won't like it, like, all these toys that he is buying them . . . the guy lending money for a homeless kid down the street. . . he bought a little 25 cents monkey that wouldn't work tomorrow, but to this little kid, it looks like he lent him enough money to buy him a house.

The other interviewees were not quite sure what the point of the toystore item was. Fifth-grade Brad thought hard in answer to the question, 'What do you think that story was about?'

Brad: I wasn't really sure what it was about. It was sort of hard to understand. He just went shopping.

Even the usually astute Lauren (fourth grade) did not understand the analogy between spending in a toy store and the national debt:

Int: Do you think they're trying to teach you anything?

Lauren: To teach kids that if you ask for money, you might get it.

One first grader, Anna, made a revealing category mistake:

Int: What was that news item telling us? Do you know what it was all about?

Anna: It was a commercial for toys.

Int: And what do commercials do?

Anna: They try to make people want to buy their things.

Thus, although the children understood the narrative of the toystore, they found the behavior of the protagonists puzzling (people don't lend other people money) because they did not grasp the underlying analogy with economic policy, where, of course, people do lend other people money. Only Ben appeared to grasp it and, significantly, he did not make the point that storekeepers don't usually lend shoppers money. This is a good example of an extended piece of televisual metaphor that only makes sense if the viewer understands the three different components of the metaphor: the topic (the government's borrowing and overspending); the vehicle (the extravagant shopper in the toy store) and the common ground (borrowing, overspending, and debt). The second-order processing required here is very extended and if the basic concept is not grasped, the different illustrations of the analogy make less and less sense, the longer the item continues—for instance, the presenter buying a toy for "a kid in hospital" and telling himself "what a nice guy I am" (an obvious allusion to softhearted liberal welfare spending).

This treatment, clever and well-worked out though it was, was an outstandingly good example of the pitfalls of trying to dress up television news with drama and humor to make it appealing for children, resulting in it being actually much less comprehensible than a straightforward explanation would have been. An intelligent child like Ben would almost certainly have got more useful information from an article in *The Wall Street Journal*. The item failed to be informative, even to these privileged and articulate viewers, because it failed to recognize the difficulty that extended metaphoric and analogic material can present. *Real News for Kids* is targeted at the age group of the older children in the study, and given that they were an untypically advantaged group, it ought to be disappointing to the producers that these bright, literate children did not understand the point they were trying to get across. The problems these children had suggest that the techniques of drama and comedy do not always mix well with those of nonfiction genres, and that, where they are combined, confusion can result. Not only was the extended metaphor not understood, but some children's attempts to categorize the program based on its surface features resulted in their not realizing the kind of program it was, as in Anna's referring to it as a commercial. Because judgments about how seriously programs should be taken can depend on what genre they are perceived to be, it seems important that news and educational programs should clearly identify themselves as such. The techniques of comedy and commerce used in a news item may detract from the information being given by suggesting that there is no need to take it seriously. This point has been made many times in studies of responses to adult news (see for instance, Jamieson, 1993), but it has particular importance for children and for media education.

When modality techniques designed to create illusion are applied appropriately by producers, as in drama programs, children's responses can be very different, as we see in chapters 9 and 10. Dramatic fiction, as in the examples of sitcom and of fantasy narrative used in the study, has codes and conventions that children are very familiar with. These children were certainly well steeped in both literary and televisual story telling, as their questionnaire responses on their TV viewing and on their reading indicated (see chapter 5). In their responses to the fiction programs, described in the following chapters, the children in my study made no category mistakes; comedy was identified as comedy, fiction as fiction, and fairy tale as fairy tale. Even where they did not understand the story (partly because the clips were incomplete), their hypotheses about what was going on were well grounded in narrative likelihood, drawing on their knowledge of the rules of art, as well as those of life.

9

"A Comedy Fiction Type of Thing": The Cosby Show

The most popular kind of programming with elementary school children, and certainly a major source of their ideas about real relationships (Dorr et al., 1990), is drama programming. In the United States, the situation comedy is the dominant dramatic form, occupying nearly all the major prime-time (6:30 to 10:00 P.M.) slots on the networks and, in syndicated rerun form, on local stations, too. Situation comedies are very tightly formatted and (particularly in the United States) made cheaply. They may have highly paid stars, such as Roseanne, or Bill Cosby (the star of the show used in the study), but most take place on one or two studio sets, with a limited cast of regular characters (usually including some children and/or adolescents) and follow a highly predictable and stylized set of formulas. As such, although they ostensibly represent real families and are naturalistic in their scripting and performance, they are, in fact, governed by rigid and recognizable rules.

In the world of U.S. sitcom, most of the limited numbers and types of characters are attractive and reasonably prosperous; people with unresolvable social problems (such as the extremely poor) are rarely featured. Neither are people from specific parts of the country. Most sitcoms have indefinable settings and no particular local accents, although one or two, such as *Seinfeld*, make a feature of being set in a particular place like New York City, despite being shot, like nearly everything else on American TV, in Hollywood. Sitcom problems are usually personal and have to be resolved happily within the space of one 24-minute episode; events have to be structured to allow three commercial breaks, each following a comic climax; there is always laughter on the soundtrack, either from a live studio audience or canned. Within this tightly artificial formula, real originality of characterization, writing, and performance can sometimes be achieved, and the rules can also be broken.

An example of such an achievement was *The Cosby Show* that, according to Gitlin (1983), single-handedly revived the sitcom format on television in 1984, and represented a creative breakthrough in its representation of African Americans on television.

> It has had potentially decisive effects in convincing middle Americans that a black man and his family can be their most favored weekly guest, reversing the tradition of *Amos 'n' Andy* in which blacks were funny because they were different, and even inferior linguistically. (Real, 1991).

In its early days, the show was also refreshingly determined to play against sentimental expectations of family relationships; there was palpable shock in the studio audience when Theo's (applauded) speech about how he expected his father's love and loyalty, despite being careless with money, was met by Cosby's line, "That's the biggest garbage I ever heard."

The third program sequence used in the study was a scene from this show—as mentioned, the first prime-time hit comedy to feature African American characters who were dramatically central (almost every character, major or minor, in the eight-year series run was black), and who were neither comic stereotypes nor people with major social problems. Interestingly, not one of our 24 interviewees—18 main study, and 6 pilot—including three black children, commented on the representation of race in *The Cosby Show* as being not real; in fact, nobody commented on it in any way. Yet the unreality of the show's representation of race has been a major discussion point between academics and critics, with some commentators arguing that *The Cosby Show* unrealistically excluded racism and its problems, and the program's defenders, including Bill Cosby himself, arguing that the show—a family sitcom, like any other—should not have to shoulder more social responsibilities than sitcoms made by white people (see e.g. Real, 1991).

The clip came from the late 1980s series in which all the Huxtable children were still living at home and the youngest child, Rudy, was around 6 years old. The scene showed Rudy and Theo, her 16-year-old brother, playing checkers and being interrupted by 14-year-old Vanessa, who was excited about being asked to join the school pep squad. The checkers scene was intercut with a scene between the two parents, Cliff (Bill Cosby) and his wife, Claire, in which Claire enlists Theo's help in trying to prevent Cliff from going to the electrical-goods store and buying a lot of gadgets (an interesting, but coincidental, parallel, with the shopaholic sequence in *Real News*). Cliff goes off to the store, and Theo and Claire telephone the store keeper and ask him not to sell Cliff anything. During the scene, Claire is seated on the sofa, masked by a very large teddy bear (which, one of the children told me later, was to disguise the fact that the actress was pregnant at the time). The scene ends with Cliff coming back from the store, having bought the gadget he went for and insisting that he was able to resist the temptation to buy other things. But the viewer, having heard Claire's phone call to the storekeeper, knows that Cliff is lying. Irony is the source of the comedy at this point, with the studio audience laughing knowingly as Bill Cosby goes into his injured innocent routine. The two scenes were shot on a studio set—kitchen and sitting room—and there was audience laughter throughout. The incidents that caused children to press pause for "couldn't happen in real life" are itemized in Table 9.1.

The Cosby Show sequence, roughly the same length as the other clips, produced very little pausing from any of the children. This was as expected, given its naturalistic style and the recognizability of its situations—siblings talking and playing games with each other, and the parents having a mild argument over one partner's shopping behavior. Counter-stereotypically, it is the father who is the irresponsible shopaholic here, but none of the children queried this. Gender, racial, class, and age stereotyping, such a central source of concern with media analysts and with college media students, such as my own, was never raised as an issue in any of the children's interviews, despite frequent and blatant examples of it, as in the case of *Sesame Street's* all-male cast of characters. As Table 9.1 shows, there were very few spontaneous presses of the pause button, and most of the children's responses to the program were in reply to the interviewers' questions after the clip had finished. None of the children

TABLE 9.1
Number of Times Events Identified as 'Not Real' in *The Cosby Show*
(Base 18, 6 in Each Age Group)

Cosby Show	All 4/5	All 3rd	All 1st	All Children	Boys	Girls
Sale prices	1	0	0	1	1	0
Teddy bear	1	0	0	1	1	0
Drs. wouldn't be at home	1	0	0	1	1	0
Laughter/clapping	2	1	0	3	2	1
Theo's timing	1	0	0	1	1	0
Humor/joke	1	0	0	1	1	0
Double jump	1	0	0	1	0	1
She couldn't beat older brother	0	1	1	2	2	0
Opponent wouldn't help	0	1	1	2	1	1
Can't buy everything in shop	0	1	0	1	0	1
Girl is lying	0	0	2	2	1	1
He didnt go to mall	0	0	1	1	1	0
Pep squad	0	0	1	1	0	1
Little girl is not funny	0	0	1	1	0	1
Total	8	4	7	19	12	7

voluntarily pointed out that it could not be real because it was drama or people acting, in the way that William (in the pilot) had done. However, Natasha (first grade) showed some awareness of scripting:

> Natasha: That little girl is not really that funny . . . They just tell her to say that.
>
> Int: Who tells her?
>
> Natasha: Producers or someone.

Awareness of the theatricality of situation comedies (which are often filmed in front of live audiences) sometimes emerged in later discussion, for example:

> Anna (first grade): I think it seemed real, but it really was just a TV show.
>
> Int: What is the difference between real and a TV show?
>
> Anna: A TV show never really happened, and it is happening on the stage. When like, someone is out, you don't see them behind the curtains.

There were three aspects of the program that prompted "couldn't happen in real life" judgments in more than one child: first, the laughter on the soundtrack (three children); second, Rudy beating Theo at checkers and Theo letting her do it (four children); and third, Cliff's less-than-truthful account of his trip to the electrical-goods store (four responses). The first was an art judgment, prompted by a special effect; the second two were life judgments, prompted by the children's knowledge and expectations of normal family behavior.

"ALL THOSE PEOPLE IN THE BACKGROUND COULDN'T REALLY BE THERE LAUGHING"

Elijah (third grade, quoted above) identified the falsity of canned laughter:

> Elijah: It has to be on stage or they put the laughing in it.
>
> Int: They put the laughing in it? How do they do that?
>
> Elijah: They record it, and they push Play.

Brad (fifth grade) & Lauren (fourth grade) pointed out the artificiality of naturalistic family conversations prompting regular laughs:

> Brad: If it happened in real life there wouldn't be people laughing at them.
>
> Lauren: It's not likely that every time you do something funny, everyone would clap.

Asked what was the point of having laughter, Lauren replied with her usual pragmatic astuteness, "It makes people laugh and enjoy the show . . . It gives them a sense that other people like the show."

Ben (fifth grade), although he did not press pause for the laughter, was able to give a complex explanation of how it was done:

> Ben: They have a studio audience and they have cards and flashes, and it signals the crowd to start clapping. . . They also signal the sound manager to put the laughter on . . . It's just a way to trick people and to believe that they are doing it live, even though they aren't.

Ben was the only subject to pick up as "couldn't happen in real life" a commonplace adult criticism of *The Cosby Show*: the point that, despite the fact that nobody ever seems to do any work, the family enjoys an enviable, leisurely consumer lifestyle. Again there was no mention of race:

> Ben (*pressing pause at the very beginning, at a shot of Claire with her teddy bear in the family sitting room*): That's not real. Dad is a doctor and Mom is a lawyer and the house is always clean. A doctor and a lawyer are not going to be in the house all the time playing with teddy bears like that. They are always going to be out doing work and stuff . . . My dad is a doctor and sometimes he doesn't come home until eleven.

CONTENTIOUS REPRESENTATIONS

This was the only example of awareness of television's social representations produced by any of the 18 interviewees. This could be because these children led protected and privileged lives and imagined that everybody else led similar lives. More would need to be known about their other sources of information on social class differences to establish this. On this point, there is a contrast with Julian Sefton-Green's discussions with British teenage interviewees and students about the modality of the show (1990). Sefton-Green was particularly concerned with the issue of race and whether "*The Cosby Show* accurately or misguidedly reflects a 'black reality' " (p.132). Hence, the remarks of his interviewees focus very much on the realism of the content, with a number of references to race:

> Melanie: I can't tell you she's a typical black American wife 'cos I don't know what they're like.

> or Nkasi: . . .it's not common to see a black middle-class family in high position.

Similarly, Buckingham's interviews about the BBC's realistic soap opera *EastEnders* (Buckingham, 1988) showed that class awareness was prevalent. It is clear that some of these references to race and class were prompted by the interviewer's questioning or the task set. This indicates a cultural difference between Britain and the United States, both in their cultural representations and in approaches to media education. British dramatic representation and British cultural life, generally, are much more overtly concerned with class differences than are American representations; working-class characters and their preoccupations are found in all categories of television drama, from prestigious single plays and films to soaps. (Black characters as central protagonists, as in *The Cosby Show*, are rare, however.) A program like the working-class, London-based *EastEnders* would not get off the ground in the United States. Indeed, it did not get off the ground in the United States, being banished to one or two PBS stations. With Granada's *Coronation Street*, the other long-running British working-class soap, set in the industrial North of England, the British broadcasters were unable even to give it away to the American networks.

There are also differences in media-education syllabuses on either side of the Atlantic. As James Brown described, in his review of media-education programs (Brown, 1993), American approaches place less stress on institutional and contextual analyses and more on textual and cognitive aspects, whereas in British curricula, social-class differences in mass-media representations are a central area of discussion. Brown pointed out that "neo-Marxist perspectives" are common in UK syllabuses. He cited the Clwyd (Wales) media-studies-unit for the training of teachers, which requires children studying for their general certificate of secondary education exams in the United Kingdom to "analyze soap operas and serials to observe how 'institutional assumptions and textual strategies serve to "position" us in relation to the messages we look at or read' . . . including developing images of various social constructs (family, the nation, housewives, etc.)" (p. 229).

If American students were to study *The Cosby Show* from this perspective, they would be expected to ask searching questions, as in Sefton-Green's examples, about how it is possible for a family that never does any work to have such high levels of conspicuous consumption, and why, in the context of the economics of American commercial network television, these questions might be unacceptable in a prime-time show. The question of racism and the extent to which it is off the agenda in a program set in New York, a city containing huge economic and racial divisions, would also be examined. Media education can thus touch on extremely contentious areas of discussion that some teachers might prefer to avoid. In the United Kingdom, they have to be tackled if they appear on national examination syllabi. They are certainly contentious, but they have become part of an accepted tradition of classroom discussion, as Buckingham's and Sefton-Green's work illustrates. Whether these neo-Marxist British approaches to media education are actually helping to reduce class differences in the United Kingdom is debatable, because social and economic inequality have increased. The political history of the country since 1979, dominated by a right-wing conservative government and supported by an increasingly right-wing popular press, suggests that educational attempts to raise class consciousness in children through deconstructing the media have not yet translated into direct political effects.

"SHE COULDN'T BEAT SOMEBODY WAY OLDER THAN HER"

Primary-school-aged children, whether American or British, tend to lead lives dominated more by family politics than by national ones. An incident that produced high levels of indignation at its unlikelihood concerned sibling relationships in *The Cosby Show*. A number of children queried the reality of the older brother allowing his younger sister to beat him at checkers, despite the fact that this was quite naturalistically scripted. Theo gave in to Rudy's manipulation out of sheer boredom, a fairly likely situation when older brothers have to amuse younger sisters. Nevertheless, this outcome was strongly resisted, and its lack of realism analyzed in some detail by the children who commented on it:

> Jack (first grade): I never knew that a little 3-year-old can beat a 17 year old.
>
> Int: Why do you suppose they have her beating the older kid at checkers?
>
> Jack: They set up the board like she was beating him and they left out the space where they wanted him to go. He went there and she double jumped him.
>
> Ruth (third grade): Nobody from the red team would tell you where to go. They would, like, block your move when it is your turn.
>
> Int: Why do you think that's happening?
>
> Ruth: She doesn't know how to play very good.

Sarah (fourth grade) showed the most mature understanding of why a scene would be deliberately set up in this apparently unlikely way:

> Sarah: In real life they wouldn't move there if they knew it was going to be a double jump.
>
> Int: So why is it done like that?
>
> Sarah: So that she can do that part where she says "king me, king me."
>
> Int: So what's the point of doing that?
>
> Sarah: Just to make something funny because it is a comedy show.

This was an example of a combined Narrative and Pragmatic judgment. The child demonstrated her understanding that it was the requirements of the story and the genre that required the unrealistic double jump to be scripted, building to the punch line, with Rudy shouting 'King me, King me!', and the audience laugh. Again, the explanation is an internal one based on the requirements of comedy (art), not an external one based on real-life expectations. Again, too, this judgment was made by an older child. The younger ones did not give these kinds of pragmatic explanations for the lack of realism.

"THAT GUY WAS LYING"

Part of the humor of this sequence came from comic irony. (Often in *The Cosby Show*, Cliff Huxtable's pretensions to being a solemn grown-up professional are played off against Bill Cosby's actual gift for playful clowning.) The irony lay in the fact that the audience knew that Cliff was not telling the truth about his buying behavior. Claire and Theo had been seen telephoning the electrical store and asking the storekeeper not to sell Cliff any extra gadgets, apart from the remote control he had gone for. When Cliff came back, unaware of the phone call, he denied that he had wanted to buy any extra gadgets and attributed compulsive buying behavior to another person in the shop. As soon as she heard this, Natasha (first grade) pressed pause:

Natasha: That guy was lying.

Int: How do you know?

Natasha: Because the boy [Theo] said it before.

Int: Why do you think he is lying?

Natasha: Because he is always lying.

Here, Natasha demonstrates the expectations of character created by long-running television series, a necessary component of tele-literacy; the writers and producers rely on this knowledge to generate humor, just as the authors of the *Growing Pains* story described in chapter 6 assumed knowledge of the characters' backgrounds and histories in order to generate the ironic comedy of the episode.

Philip (first grade) thought that probably all the characters, including Claire, were lying, but he also recognized that this could happen in real life. This judgment required metarepresentation (Moore & Frye, 1991): the ability to understand the deceptive actions of others and, further, to recognize that such deceptions, although resting on untruths, are, at the level of experience, real, they could occur in life. Such metarepresentational awareness was also demonstrated by Sarah's acceptance of the necessity of allowing a younger child to beat an older one in the artistic interests of comic effect. Tim (fifth grade) thought it unlikely that someone would "pay regular prices if they were on sale" (referring to Cliff's burning desire to own as many electrical gadgets as possible, regardless of price). In general, however, *The Cosby Show* prompted very few judgments of events that 'couldn't happen in real life.'

Ruth (third grade) explained why she had not pressed pause very much during the Cosby clip, and her explanation can stand for the other children's unquestioning acceptance of its general naturalism:

> Ruth: A lot of that could have happened in real life. . . I mean like playing checkers, you could have gotten beaten by somebody that is learning how to play. I mean somebody could want to pay regular prices for something on sale. So most of them could have happened in real life.

10

"It's Supposed to Be a Fairytale": The Sand Fairy

The final sequence used was from the BBC's 1992 adaptation of *Five Children and It* by Edith Nesbit, shown in 1993 on The Disney Channel as *The Sand Fairy*. The production was a costume drama set in Nesbit's own Edwardian era. It was of interest to discover that none of the children had seen or heard of the program or of the book, and, despite being in very book-oriented schools, neither had their teachers. This was an unexpected advantage in that the children had no preconceptions at all about what was going on, and they were able to construct interpretations of their own. An opportunity was created to see if there was a crossover of literacy skills from book reading, to reading television, in order to activate schemata based on other experiences of fantasy fiction, the process described by Susan Neumann in her work on literacy and television (see chapter 4).

The Sand Fairy sequence opened with one of the four child characters suddenly materializing in a room in a besieged castle turret, where he and his three siblings had found themselves as a result of a wish. This wish, that their house could be a medieval castle, had earlier been granted by the Psammead (the eponymous fairy). A complication of the situation was that, as a result of earlier wishes going rather badly wrong, the children had requested that nobody except themselves would notice the outcome of their wishes. Hence, the castle was invisible to the household servants, who carried on their duties using invisible (to the viewer) utensils and tools. The sequence included an exploration of the castle accompanied by atmospheric music, and ended with a particularly realistic overlay effect of the children's baby brother apparently floating in mid-air, while really sitting in his high-chair. This caused great alarm to the sister who found him.

The Sand Fairy was a classic BBC children's drama, shot on location in a real castle, with generous production values including the use of a troop of knights in armor with real horses. For American children, it contained a number of potentially puzzling distancing characteristics: first, the English speech and locations; second the dual (and probably unfamiliar) historical references. The Edwardian era is a period with plenty of American iconography of its own; costumes and props of the period would be familiar to American children from TV shows like *Anne of Green Gables, The Little House on the Prairie*, and *Avonlea*. But *The Sand Fairy* superimposed a medieval setting onto the Edwardian one, and (*pace* Disneyland) cultural reference points from the Middle Ages are far less available to American children than to English ones. There are no authentic medieval castles within about 3,000 miles of Philadelphia.

The narrative complexity of the sequence presented a considerable challenge. Not only was the scene taken from the middle of the story, so that the children had very little idea of what was going on, but it also used three separate groups of characters (children, servants, knights) clad in three different kinds of costume, simultaneously taking part in two separate sets of actions, supposedly separated by about 400 years in time, with the child protagonists bridging the two. Its special invisibility effects were very convincing and presented further problems of interpretation. The point of view of the narrative was the point of view of the child protagonists: thus, the servants could not see the castle or the knights in armor, and the knights could not see the servants, but we (the audience) could. Because the servants' utensils were invisible to the child characters, they were presented as invisible to the viewers. This required the actors playing the servants to mime. The effect of the invisible highchair, on the other hand, was an electronic effect achieved by the use of chromakey—the baby was not miming.

This short sequence required several shifts in point of view, signaled by a variety of production techniques. The servants were not aware of the point of view of the child protagonists (shared by the audience), and they showed impatience at the behavior of the four increasingly panic-stricken children. Similarly, the medieval knights were completely unaware of the fact that they were really besieging a desirable detached residence in the Edwardian Home Counties. Thus, they insisted on treating the strangely dressed (to them) child protagonists as spies. The comic effect of all this depended on the child audience being able to see the situation from both the children's and the other characters' perspectives. The complexity created by television's special narrative and technological devices (and, to give Nesbit her due, by the original author's considerable talent for farce) gave rise to some very intelligent speculations on the part of the child interviewees. It is difficult to think of a print-based task that could have brought forth the following, for example:

Lauren (fourth grade girl) (after pressing the pause button at the floating baby): No one really floats like that. . .

Int: How is that done?

Lauren: They have attached clear ropes that you can't see or ropes with certain colors that can't be seen by film. . . If it was a high chair you would be able to see it. . . But there is obviously something going on because he [the baby] is just floating in thin air and she doesn't notice it.

Int: Who doesn't notice it?

Lauren: The maid.

Int: How do you know she is a maid?

Lauren: Because of the clothes that she was wearing and what she was doing.

Int.: Which was?

Lauren: She was doing the cooking and stuff like that.

Table 10.1 (opposite) shows the events identified as not real in *The Sand Fairy* clip. Twenty events prompted the pressing of the pause button, by far the largest number of all the clips; in *Sesame Street* and *Real News* only 12 events each led to button-pressing. (On the other hand, more children pressed pause in *Sesame Street*, which meant that the overall total of pauses was greater—81 to *The Sand Fairy*'s 68.)

"SOMEBODY JUST CAN'T COME OUT OF THIN AIR"

The very first event in *The Sand Fairy* clip was a piece of special effects magic (a word used by a number of children in connection with special effects) that the children had to be very vigilant to spot; four of the first graders did not spot it, but all except one child in the older two age groups did. It was a scene in which one of the four children in the story suddenly materialized in a castle turret where his three siblings were waiting for him. It aroused almost universal skepticism:

Natasha (first grade): You can't just appear like that.

Suzanne (third grade): He appeared out of nowhere!

Ryan (third grade): I don't think he would really come right out of thin air.

Eve (fourth grade): You just don't rise up like that.

Lauren (fourth grade): Stop there! No one can appear like that.

Brad (fifth grade): He wouldn't have appeared like that.

Sarah (fourth grade): A person couldn't come out of thin air.

Int: Why not?

Table 10.1
Number of Times Events Identified as Not Real in *The Sand Fairy*

Sand Fairy	All 4/5	All 3rd	All 1st	All Children	Boys	Girls
Sudden appearance	5	6	2	13	6	7
Not medieval	1	0	0	1	1	0
Wrong light	1	0	0	1	1	0
Invisible objects	4	5	3	12	4	8
Baby flying	6	6	7	19	10	9
Cutaway to knights	2	0	0	2	1	1
Different set (castle)	1	0	0	1	1	0
Wouldn't blow horn	1	1	0	2	1	1
Entry time wrong	1	0	0	1	1	0
Background music	2	1	1	4	1	3
Wishs don't come true	2	0	0	2	0	2
Knights' swords	1	0	1	2	0	2
Bows & arrows	1	0	0	1	0	1
War not in house	0	1	0	1	0	1
Sound effects	0	1	0	1	0	1
Noise in sword	0	0	1	1	1	0
Not real army	0	0	1	1	1	0
Not real castle	0	0	1	1	1	0
Hanging from window	0	0	1	1	0	1
Stairs too tight	0	0	1	1	0	1
Total	28	21	19	68	30	38

Sarah: Because people can't disappear and reappear.

Int: How do you know?

Sarah: Because nobody ever does that.

Int: So what's the point of doing it here?

Sarah: It is supposed to be a fairy tale.

Here, it is an older girl again who is able to articulate her real-world experience that people do not reappear and disappear, but she is also able to articulate her knowledge of literary conventions and to point out that, within the fairy-tale genre such things are possible. Lauren (fourth grade) used a similar explanation: "It's probably a fiction thing about magic." Like the fifth grade boys, Brad, Tim, and Ben, Lauren had a good idea of how the effect was done:

Lauren: First they clip it without him, and they stop it, and then they put him in and they start it again. [Who are they?] The people on the camera.

But the younger children demonstrated some interesting confusions between the representation of magic using editing techniques and the idea of magic itself. Third graders seemed to be at an intermediate stage between a mature rational awareness of technique and a lingering childish need to believe in the supernatural (as with the questionnaire data about Santa Claus). For instance:

Int: Why do you think he appears out of nowhere?

Suzanne (third grade): Because he is in time travel.

Int: How do you think they have done that?

Suzanne: They used the time machine and he disappeared and appeared. They shot one scene with the time machine there, and then they stopped and moved it, and then he appeared.

Paul (third grade): It's like a ghost or something captured by a spell.

First graders (despite frequent references to magic) demonstrated some robust common sense in trying to understand the puzzling occurrences of the story:

Natasha: Maybe there is something under the thing that goes down and you can push it up [A trap door].

Philip: When he says *The Sand Fairy*, there's probably not a real fairy.

The questionnaire data about first graders' belief in Santa Claus suggests that this kind of remark from younger children indicates an acceptance of such things as "real fairies"; Philip could be making a distinction here between them and the kinds of represented pretend fairies shown here in a TV drama, rather than casting doubt on the existence of fairies altogether.

"EVERYTHING IS BEING INVISIBLE"

Along with the disappearing and reappearing boy (13 pauses), and the floating baby (19 pauses, about which more will be discussed), the other large group of pauses (12) was for the use of invisible objects. This was somewhat different from the disappearance and floating effects; the disappearance and the floating effects were achieved electronically, as a number of the older children were able to explain. But the invisibility effect was created by the actors, who mimed various tasks as if they were using irons and cooking pots. This variety of illusions prompted a number of literate speculations in the children and revealed some age differences in the way the children tried to account for these illusions. As before, first graders tended to resort to magic:

> Anna: It looks like she is holding something but she really isn't.
>
> Int: So what is going on?
>
> Anna: Everything is being invisible.
>
> Int: Is it? Why do you think that is?
>
> Anna: The Sand Fairy.
>
> Joe: She can't just go out and pour without her hand - that could be in the future.
>
> Int: What made you think it was in the future?
>
> Joe: Because they didn't have that so they used something else . . . the future has real good magic things.

These explanations do not necessarily mean that these 6- and 7-year-olds believed in magic or in time travel in real life. However, where the invisible objects were concerned, their answers were distinguished from older children's by being based on the internal premises of the story, which is "a fairy tale." For instance, first-grade Philip paused the tape when he saw, through the shocked eyes of one of the girl characters, the image of the floating baby, and said, "She's probably dreaming. It's not a real baby flying." In other words, his explanation for the flying baby being not real was based on the perspective of the fictional character; it wasn't real to her, it must have been in her dream. External explanations based on knowledge of production and performance techniques, such as "she's pretending" or "she's acting" were not invoked by the first graders, whereas among older children they were:

> Elijah (third grade): She didn't [really] stir anything because she didn't have a spoon.
>
> Louise (third grade): The person wasn't really doing anything with that. There was no thread and that person didn't have anything in her hand or anything she was doing. She was just holding her hand like that.

However, older children, too, when asked for further explanations of why and how these effects were created, sometimes resorted to internal explanations based on the story as they saw it, rather than to "they" or "he" or "she," meaning the real-world actors and producers (as already discussed). This perhaps suggests the power of convincingly acted fairy tales to foster the suspension of disbelief. Children were more likely to enter into the internal world of the story in this fashion when the effects were created by performance, than when they were created by electronic techniques, which is not necessarily what one would expect in an age where more and more convincing "virtual reality" is displacing traditional television-drama production methods. For instance, Tim (fifth grade) who frequently referred to "special effects in the studio," also referred to magic when asked about the invisibility effect;

Tim: She has nothing in her hands.

Int: Why do you think she has nothing in her hands?

Tim: Because they are magical items or something.

Sarah (fourth grade) also used internal explanations:

Those people [referring to the maids] are doing something but the things they are doing aren't there. Things that they are working on aren't there.

Int: So where are they?

Sarah: Probably in the castle.

Int: So what is the explanation of doing things with things that aren't there? [expecting the answer, "she's acting"]

Sarah: The things that they were working on may have just disappeared like that boy disappeared.

In Sarah's case, this conversation about the invisibility effect led to an incisive recognition of the different points of view of the protagonists:

Int: Who in the story can see those things?

Sarah: I think she can.

Int: Who can?

Sarah: The girl. No, no! The people can.

Int: I see.

Sarah: She can't.

"THE BABY IS FLYING!"

As mentioned, the flying-baby event along with the blocks moving by themselves in *Sesame Street* was one of only two events to be unanimously voted "Couldn't happen in real life." Explanations of why not, as with the blocks, tended to get mixed up with explanations of how the effect was achieved:

Philip (first grade): It's not a real baby flying.

Int: How do you know?

Philip: Because how can a baby fly?

Int: How would they make it look like it's flying?

Philip: They probably have a rope around her, like a string, a strong string, and they pull and make her go.

Age differences again appeared in reasons for the impossibility of this event, with the youngest children invoking magic (or at least science fiction—Joe's favored explanations for a number of things), older ones referring to human biology, and the oldest group stressing special effects as reasons:

Joe (first grade): A lady can't be falling in the air.

Int: Why not?

Joe: Because they have to in outer space, but they won't breathe, so they'll die.

Ruth (third grade): Nobody can just float in thin air?

Int: Why?

Ruth: If you are floating in thin air, why do people have legs?

Lauren, (fourth grade): No one really floats like that. They have attached clear ropes that you can't see, or ropes that have certain colors that can't be seen by film.

As with the blocks, a number of children resorted to the idea of ropes or strings to account for real-world objects doing things that they should not be able to do. But Ben (fifth grade) knew the real answer:

Ben: That's fake. They say a baby's just floating there.

Int: And how is it done?

Ben: A technique called green screen. They put everything else in green and they put the baby there. And they place the green in that film with the background, so it looks like it's [floating], and it really isn't.

"THAT WOULDN'T HAPPEN IN MEDIEVAL TIMES"

The excerpt from *The Sand Fairy* required children to activate a number of schemata about history and the past because it was quite clearly not set in the present day. Although several of the children articulated a sense of historical action, none of them was able to articulate the double time period, Edwardian and medieval, although a few mentioned time travel.

A number of comments expressed a sense of period, even if a somewhat shaky one in the case of the youngest children:

> Jack (first grade): It was like in the olden days. It was like a castle, kind of, like sometimes in fairy tales they have castles.

> Joe (first grade): That could be in the future . . . they didn't have that [referring to the invisible objects] so they used something else. . ... The future has real good magic things.

Elijah (third grade) speculated directly on when the program was meant to be happening:

> Elijah: It was like early 1800s.

> Int: What gave you that idea?

> Elijah: Because of the background and stuff and the clothes that they were wearing.

Eve (fourth grade) also placed the program's setting in the 1800s, which is a reasonably accurate guess at the period of the Edwardian costumes of the children, but again, like Elijah, Eve did not identify the action as taking place in two different historical periods:

> Eve: I wouldn't look out my window and find people with swords, but that was in the olden days.

> Int: What do you mean olden days? When do you think this was made?

> Eve: Made? The 1990s.

> Int: When do you think it is supposed to be? What period?

> Eve: Probably in the 1800s.

Fourth grade Lauren was one of the most stimulating of the interviewees. Because her opinions were invariably interesting, and because she seemed to enjoy giving them, the opportunity was taken to probe her sense of the different time periods of the story in some detail:

> Lauren (pausing the tape): No kids would shoot bows and arrows.

> Int: Why is that not real?

> Lauren: Are you talking about now? Because it is back in the medieval times and it couldn't happen now. . ... It could happen in earlier times. Well, not the magic part, but having the knights and stuff.

> Int: So what are you saying?

> Lauren: It's the past.

Int: And when was the program made?

Lauren: When was it supposed to be taking place?

Int: OK, tell me when it was supposedly taking place.

Lauren: In the medieval times.

Int: And how do you know that?

Lauren: Because of the knights and armor and the way the horses were clothed and stuff like that.

Int: What about the children?

Lauren: And the clothes that they were wearing?

Int: Are they medieval clothes?

Lauren: Yeah.

Int: But is it taking place in medieval times?

Lauren: Yeah.

Int: Was the program made in medieval times?

Lauren: No. Present.

Int: How do you know that?

Lauren: They taped it. You don't know?

Int: That's what I am trying to get at. You're not saying it was made then?

Lauren: Yeah.

Int: OK. So who are these people?

Lauren: They're actors.

Because Lauren seemed so tele-literate, I checked her writing fluency in the questionnaire answers, particularly the open-ended section where she was required to explain how television pictures change. Her written account gives little hint of the kind of reasoning she was able to display in her interview. Here it is (with authentic spelling):

> They stop the film and, take away and, add what they need then the start the camera again and it look like it just disapeared or apeared.

Admittedly, children (or indeed adults) do not do their best literary writing when they are hurrying through a questionnaire, but this gives no suggestion of the quality and detail of Lauren's comments about the TV clips; possibly she is a girl who expresses herself better orally. Nevertheless, I hope she gets the opportunity to develop the kinds of perceptions and insights she showed when talking about television programs in her interview at other points in her school career, if not by talking about television, then perhaps through drama or film criticism.

"YOU NEVER KNOW IF THERE WOULD BE GERMS ON IT"

There were a number of points at which children stopped the tape in order to demonstrate a rather superior modern disapproval for the way the children in the story—which was in "olden times"—were behaving:

> Ben (fifth grade): (seeing a shot of the four children looking out of a turret window): People won't look out of a window like that, especially then because you can easily fall down.
>
> Anna (first grade): People don't usually hang out windows because they can get killed.
>
> Ruth (fourth grade): If you would just pick up an old horn and blow on it, you would never know if there would be germs on it.

"THAT CASTLE IS FAKE"

It was also quite difficult for the children to believe that there are such things as authentic historical settings that could be used as a realistic backdrop for a fictional tale. The castle (a real one) aroused skepticism:

> Ben (fifth grade): It is all a different set. They're not doing this in the big castle like that.
>
> Int: Then what are they trying to do?
>
> Ben: They're just trying to express to you that this film is supposed to be set in a castle, but you know that it really isn't.

First-grade Philip was determined not to be taken in by any of the costly and authentic production values:

> Philip: The castle is not made out of bricks; it would cost too much money to get all the bricks and all that kind of stuff.

Not only was the castle seen to be inauthentic, but the accents of the characters were also seen to be similarly fake:

> Philip (first grade): They're real American people but they have an accent though.
>
> Int: So which country do you think it is in?
>
> Philip: Probably England or something like that . . .. You know how they have accents the people? Probably it's not like an accent, it's not really their

accent. It's like someone, probably like you know the things that you put in your mouth and it makes you change your voice.

Similar cynicism was shown by third-grade Elijah:

Int: Where do you think the program was made?

Elijah: In Universal Studios.

I suspect that different answers would have been given by English children about the setting and the period. (The shortness of the time period for the research did not permit a British version of the study, which would have been desirable.) English child viewers are very familiar with children's television drama with real historical settings shot on location. Adaptations of classics such as *Oliver Twist* and *Little Lord Fauntleroy*; modern historical novels and screenplays, such as Leon Garfield's; many TV series stories based on Robin Hood or on Roman Britain have all taken advantage of the availability of historic sites in Britain. Medieval towns like Sandwich, stately homes like Castle Howard, or prehistoric stone circles such as Avebury, have served as a backdrop for scores of TV series. The historical associations of such settings is often reinforced for children by items on children's magazine shows, such as the BBC's *Blue Peter*. Here, in addition to giving children information about the history of the place and the modern technology used to transform it, broadcasting organizations like the BBC can intelligently advertise their own products and build and maintain loyal audiences for future adult programs. Children raised on *Oliver Twist* are primed for *Middlemarch*.

The confident skepticism of these Philadelphia children about the authenticity of the settings was a surprise; they seemed to be convinced that almost the whole physical environment depicted on TV was fake—a favorite word. This is a reflection on the cheap production values of much prime-time television, where the shakiness of the sets is only too evident. Possibly, too, they are true children of post-modernism and have learned the lessons of self-conscious deconstruction provided by programs like *Growing Pains* and *Moonlighting*. Nevertheless, there is no evidence that this cynicism detracted from the children's perception of the authenticity of the story and their understanding of what it was saying. As already commented, the suspension of disbelief was preserved intact in many of their explanations of the story's events. British television prides itself on loving attention to accurate period detail (what one critic has called "the Thirties cardigan school of design"), but, as child interviewees have repeatedly demonstrated in this and other studies, children's criteria of authenticity are not necessarily the same as adult criteria. Given that this was a drama, artificial sets in a studio could actually appear more honest by these children's standards than using authentic locations. After all, Castle Howard is somebody's home; why stage a dramatic performance in it?

"IT HELPS YOU GET A FEEL OF WHAT'S GOING ON"

Music and sound effects (as when the "germ-ridden" horn was blown) were an integral part of the dramatization of the events shown in this scene and several children mentioned them, for instance Jack (first grade):

> Jack: You can't blow into a horn and make that noise . . .. They had some kind of special instrument and he just put the sword in his mouth and pretended that he blew. When he blew, someone else blew some instrument.

Music was recognized by a number of children as having an important artistic and narrative function. Their comments about its use illustrate particularly clearly the combination of pragmatic understanding and aesthetic awareness required for literate interpretations of fantasy drama, for example:

> Natasha (first grade): When they have the music it makes you think that something bad is going to happen.
>
> Int: So she is looking in the suit of armor and the music makes you think . . .
>
> Natasha: It is scary or something.

And star interviewee Lauren (fourth grade):

> Lauren: Stop! You really don't have music playing in real life.
>
> Int: So where is that coming from?
>
> Lauren: From speakers to make the effects more realistic.
>
> Int: And what is the effect?
>
> Lauren: Different kinds of music. Some music makes it suspenseful and it tells you when something exciting is going to happen.
>
> Int: And what is this music?
>
> Lauren: This music is like hurrying and trying to get where they are going and they are trying to find things. It also helps you to get a feel of what's going on.

This last comment sums up succinctly the way in which artistic production features of a piece of film or television can cue the viewer in to making judgments about the reality status of the story or information, he or she is being given. The reality status of the content, as these children's comments have frequently made clear, is not just a question of the relationship of art to life—of formal features of the medium to the real world outside the TV set. It is also a more subtle relationship—a metarepresentational one—between what ought to be real within the terms of the story and what is actually happening in the way this particular story is being told. These kinds of judgments do not permit Ts to "mark the spot" for buried treasure; they question whether *The Sand Fairy* is an accurate representation of "a real fairy." They draw attention to the ways in which music can indicate something bad or scary. They point out that, despite the fact that real brothers do not allow their young sisters to "double jump" them, the demands of situation comedy make such an event feasible. Such judgments are a combination of judgments drawn from scientific and cultural knowledge, real-world experience, experience of stories, television and film, and individual hypotheses and speculations drawn from children's own private worlds and fantasies, some of which obviously came from cultural experiences like stories, books, and films, others of which came from their own imaginations.

11

Modality: Conversations About the Relationship of Art to Life

The interviews included a number of follow-up questions after the children had initially identified something "that could not happen in real life" and paused the tape. These follow-up probes gave rise to more extended conversations about TV reality and its relationship to art and life. The number of modality references made by each child in these conversations were noted and itemized and they appear in the taxonomy shown in Figure 5.1 (page 54). Some statistical analyses were done that suggest a relationship between pragmatic judgments and prosocial judgements and some age differences in the kinds of references to production features made by the children (see chapter 5).

A conversation about TV reality with bright 6- to 11-year olds cannot be contained within the boundaries of statistical analysis, and the process of identifying specific kinds of reference in order to quantify them, does not give a full flavor of the children's reasoning any more than trying to quantify children's conversations at home would do. The model for the interview procedure in this study was a conversation between my-11-year old daughter and me as we watched *Growing Pains*. We discussed the ways in which it played with our perceptions of reality and fantasy, particularly in the way it challenged us to work out what was real life and what was fiction. This episode of the sitcom (as described in chapter 6), somewhat subversively—and in the excellent company of the authors of *A Midsummer Night's Dream* and *La Vida es Sueno*—suggested that fiction was real and life was not. It was an example of how popular art can act as a stimulus to media and literary education within the home, and almost certainly does in millions of homes, as Bianculli (1992) documented.

In this chapter, some further examples are given of different kinds of modality references to illustrate the terms used in the study. Then, examples of more extended conversations are given, to illustrate the relationships between the different categories. As has been said repeatedly, it is impossible to pull apart the categories of life and art, or form and content, or external and internal (other researchers' terminologies) in evaluating viewers' modality judgments. When people make judgments about art and the way in which it represents life, they must draw on the artistic features of the work itself in order to evaluate its verisimilitude. These children's extended comments make this point clear, if it has not already been made so.

LIFE, ART, AUTHORS, AUDIENCES

The different modality references produced by the 18 interviews broke down, as in the case of earlier researchers such as Liebes and Katz (1990) and Buckingham (1993a), into two broad categories of life and art (Buckingham's external and internal). That is, some judgments about the reality or unreality of the material were based on the children's real-world knowledge and experience (life/external) and others were based on references to technical and formal aspects of the medium (art/internal). Within these two major groups were a number of subcategories. The life group had two subcategories: the first, labeled Impossible, consisted of references to violations of natural and scientific laws, mostly related to the behavior of objects, but sometimes to human beings (e.g., "people can't float in the air"). The second life category, labeled Improbable, referred to implausible and unlikely human behavior.

Within the art group there was a greater number of subcategories, no doubt partly as a function of the choice of stimulus material, which had more than its fair share of special effects and formal production styles. (Nevertheless, it would not be untypical of an evening's viewing children could expect to be exposed to all these features and more during an average day.) These, to some extent, were analogues to Bazalgette's categories in primary media education (1988). There were four main art categories:

1. Effects (Bazalgette's Technology);
2. Theater, aspects of performance, dressing up, staging, and so on (partly Bazalgette's Representation, but also Languages and Technology);
3. Genre (Bazalgette's Categories);
4. Narrative (Language)

There were two further small groups of reference that did not quite fit into the categories above: Magic and Aesthetic. Aesthetic comments were references to the aesthetic function, quality and emotional effect of various production features such as music. The aesthetic references could be spread across all the above categories because they were usually made in conjunction with some aspect of production, performance, or audience impact, but again, they constituted a distinct type of reference of their own. Because they were not produced by all the children who commented on formal features, they were considered to merit a separate category. The term magic was used in connection with special effects effects, but the term was used sufficiently often by the younger children to justify its being separately itemized.

These different categories and subcategories of modality judgment are arranged schematically in Table 11.1.

Brief examples of comments from each category are given next:

Life

Impossible : Based on Scientific Knowledge About the Laws of Physics or Biology in the Natural World

Jack (First-grade boy): The blocks can't move themselves.

Ruth (Third-grade girl): You couldn't go under water like that and make funny faces.

Elijah (Third-grade boy; referring to rapid cutting from one person to another, each one talking about Ross Perot in *Real News for Kids*): They couldn't go from all those people that fast.

Improbable: Implausible Human Behavior

Sarah (Fourth-grade girl; referring to the phone ringing): That kind of thing could happen but really it wouldn't. It could be a coincidence.

TABLE 11.1
Levels of Modality: Categories Produced by Children's Interviews Grouped
According to Real World References (LIFE) and Production/Formal References (ART).

1st order	LIFE		ART			
	Impossible	Improbable	Effects (Magic) (Aesthetic)	Theater	Genre	Narrative
2nd order	P R A		G M A T I C			
	Pragmatic		Prag/Effects Prag/Art		Prag/Genre	Prag/Narr

Anna (First-grade girl; referring to *Real News for Kids*): People don't usually give other people money.

Paul (Third-grade boy; referring to *The Cosby Show*): She couldn't beat somebody way older than her.

Ben (Fifth-grade boy referring to *The Cosby Show*): That's not real. Dad is a doctor and Mom is a lawyer and the house is always clean.

Art

Effects: Based on technological "tricks" of the medium

Jack (First-grade boy): The baby was sitting on air.

Int: Why do you think they had the baby sitting on air like that?

Jack: Maybe they had like a mirror chair and he might have been like on a chair and that is probably how he did it. Maybe some of it was a computer.

Elijah (Third grade boy): He didn't run that fast.

Int: So what's happening there?

Elijah: They're doing something with the camera. They're doing something special with the picture.

Lauren (Fourth-grade girl; referring to speeded up action in *Real News*): He couldn't really go that fast. They are speeding up the film and they're making the clip go faster.

Int: Any reason do you think?

Lauren: Because they have to fit it all into one time slot.

Tim (Fifth-grade boy; referring to the telephone voice in *Sesame Street*): Don't you think they have her talking fast?

Int: And why do you think they have her talking fast?

Tim: Well, in a lot of movies they come out fast. He probably can't get a word in because she is talking fast . . . .Fast motion effects aren't really special. . . .Because special are effects that are, like, major effects. Like the Terminator putting his hand through a door. This was just a fast forward.

Theater: References to Performance, Staging, etc.

Elijah (Third-grade boy): Those people in the background couldn't really be there laughing. It has to be on stage or they put the laughing in it.

Anna (First-grade girl): A TV show never really happened and it is happening on the stage. When like someone is out, you don't see them behind the curtains.

Ben (Fifth-grade boy; referring to the ad for Swanns Crossing dolls before *Real News*): Those sets in the background don't come with it. Actually the kids don't make it. The adults on the crew and maintenance make it.

Genre

Int: What kind of a program was that?

Louise (Third-grade girl) A fairy tale.

Int: A fairy tale?

Louise: Something that is not true. The way the child stayed up in the air and the way they had the war and stuff.

Int: How is that one different from the one that we saw before?

Louise: That one is more mysterious and wondering what's going to happen and *The Cosby Show* is more of a comedian thing.

Int: Why have you pressed?

Philip (First-grade boy): Because it's usually an X.

Int: So you don't think there are any hidden treasures?

Anna (Fourth-grade girl): No. There would be an X if there was.

Narrative

Lauren (Fourth-grade girl; referring to the floating baby in the high chair in *The Sand Fairy*): There is obviously something going on, because he is just floating in thin air and she doesn't notice it.

Aesthetic/Art: References to Quality & Aesthetic Impact

Natasha (First-grade girl; pausing the tape at the ads for dolls): They're just trying to make it look better.

Louise (Third-grade girl; pausing the tape at the music in *The Sand Fairy*): The sound effects from the music.

Int: Why do you suppose they put the music in there?

Louise: Because they wanted to make it look like there is a mystery or something is going to happen.

Jack (First-grade boy): I thought it was going to be a scary one when they went down there and I started to like it. When I saw the guy jump out of nowhere I thought it was going to be pretty bad. It was good, but it was a lot of special effects on that one.

Magic

Int: How do you think they have him suddenly appear here?

Jack (First-grade boy): Maybe magic or a trick. Maybe they made a whole glass box but it was a mirror and you can see the guy.

Joe (First-grade boy): The future has real good magic things.

Int: How did they do that?

Ruth (Third-grade girl): The magic of TV.

Pragmatic

Int (referring to speeded up motion in *Sesame Street*): Why is it done like that?

Ryan (Third-grade boy): So it would get your attention.

Pragmatic Narrative

Sarah (Fourth-grade girl; referring to the checkers in *The Cosby Show*): In real life they wouldn't move there if they knew it was going to be a double jump.

Int: So why is it done like that?

Sarah: So that she can do the part where she says "king me, king me."

Int: So what's the point of doing that?

Sarah: Just to make something funny because it is a comedy show. (This last comment is an example of pragmatic awareness of the requirements of genre, Pragmatic/Genre.)

Pragmatic/Art

Int: Why do you think they put the music there?

Brad (Fifth-grade boy): So it helps to know what's going to happen.

Pragmatic/Effects

Lauren (Fourth-grade girl; referring to a montage of Ross Perot clips): People are all over the country and they have to use special equipment to get them all together.

Int: What is the point of doing that?

Lauren: To tell you all the different views and what everyone is talking about . . . You can get people from all over the world and tape them and bring them back to where you're shooting the actual video.

Int: Why are they speeding it up?

Lauren: It makes people want to watch it because it just does. It gets in people's minds in the way they use graphics in that show and the special effects.

Pragmatic/Genre (an interesting misattribution of genre)

Int: what was that news item all about?

Anna (First-grade girl): It was a commercial for toys.

Int: And what do commercials do?

Anna: They try to make people want to buy their things.

Ben (Fifth-grade boy; referring to *Sesame Street*): That is a program for children, preschoolers, toddlers 2 through 6, who are learning the basics: letters, numbers, shapes, like all that, how to be friends, sex, um caring.

LITERARY JUDGMENTS

As would be expected, given the study's operating assumption that modality judgments about television are literary judgments, three out of the four major categories first listed are judgments that could apply to other literary forms. Only the effects category comprised events that were exclusive to electronic media, like computer graphics, animation, and electronic sound. Theater, genre, and narrative judgments could all be equally applied to plays, live theatrical performances, and stories, and probably had been in the children's experiences of these things. This is also true of the small aesthetic group of judgments about artistic impact. Magic was invoked by children when something remarkable and unrealistic happened that they could not explain. The category of magic—perhaps appropriately—crosses the divide between art and life, between text, performance, and electronic image. It represents the mysterious power of artistic representations to look like life but not be life, and also, in the case of effects like speeded-up motion, to transform life. (Maybe young children are not so naive in using this term: I once sat in on the production of a BBC radio drama starring Robert Stephens, and whenever something worked particularly well—voice, music, sound effects—the producer referred to it as "a magic moment." Because the production was J. R. R. Tolkien's *Lord of the Rings*, the term was even more apposite.)

The final group of references were pragmatic (Bazalgette's Agency and Audience categories)—inferences and attributions showing awareness of producers' intentions, speculation about why and how things were done, and likely impact on audiences. Some of these were straightforward pragmatic awareness of somebody else being involved—simple references to "they." Others were made in conjunction with a particular production feature and were thus put in a combined category: pragmatic/effects; pragmatic/genre; pragmatic/narrative; and pragmatic/art. There is no pragmatic/theater category because this is a tautology. By showing an awareness of performance, costume, and setting, children were already demonstrating that they were aware of the constructed nature of what they were seeing and hearing. However, as already commented in discussing children's comments about the drama *The Sand Fairy*, the power of performance seemed to suspend disbelief more effectively than other formal features; references to actions such as miming, often remained within the context of the narrative rather than outside it, as when children speculated about the whereabouts of invisible objects while understanding that the actors were only pretending to use these objects.

Pragmatic judgments frequently go beyond comments about representation and effects (What and How) to ask Why? and To what end? They are second-order judgments requiring children to think on more than one level and to use embedded processes of metarepresentational reasoning. However, in evaluating the mental states of fictional characters, there are further layers of complexity, deserving of further discussion in the "theories of mind" literature. One child pointed out (about Bill Cosby/Cliff Huxtable) that his nonexistent fictional character's position was false, and that, therefore, the other nonexistent characters around him were being deceived. When this child, first-grade Natasha, said, "That guy is always lying," she did not mean that he was lying to us, that is, to her or to the television audience. She meant that he was lying to the other characters in the show, who were, as she fully understood, not real people. This kind of judgment requires a number of levels of reasoning embedded in the initial assessment (1) that the show is a fiction. Next (2) is the assessment that the fictional person in the show is making a false statement. Then (3) comes the implication that the other fictional people around this fictional lying person are being deceived; and finally, although Natasha did not make this point explicit, (4) Bill Cosby's performance as a liar was not quite convincing.

This child was 8 years old, the point at which developmental linguistic theory proposes that metalinguistic skills are developed. Because much of the research on children's theories of mind and on metalinguistic development has been done with preschoolers and kindergarten-aged children, there would seem to be scope for further research with these younger age groups into the theories they have about fictional experiences, and how such experiences inform their views of the real world. This brings us back to the question posed at the very beginning of this book by my

3-year-old traveling companion: What is a real train? And what did he mean by *real*?

SPECULATING ABOUT REALITY: CHILDREN'S CONVERSATIONS

Invitations, as in these interviews, to comment on the reality status of television or other media features inevitably produce chains of speculation that cannot be fully represented by being broken down into discrete categories, as I have here. Many of the interviewees enjoyed the conversations they were having about why programs were or were not real, how effects were achieved, and why they thought these effects had been used. Part of the process of searching for explanations and theories about TV's reality status required children to reveal their assumptions about what producers are up to and what audiences might think. Virtually no modality feature identified by the children was touched on in isolation. Nearly all the explanations and elaborations offered by the children showed an awareness of the constructed nature of TV, and an awareness of the necessity of such constructions in order for the producers to reach their goals of educating preschoolers, or making people laugh, or informing, or entertaining, or mystifying them. Most of the examples given so far are divorced from their conversational context in order to illustrate a metalinguistic point. However, it is impossible to give a proper flavor of the children's reasoning without quoting some exchanges in full.

THEORIES ABOUT SPECIAL EFFECTS

As with earlier research studies, the most frequently chosen unreal feature was special effects, but the same effects produced contrasting speculations in the children. Hence, from a critical-viewing-skills perspective, it is important to be aware that individual children have different ways of exercising critical viewing, each of which may be valid:

> Philip (referring to the change of shape in the globe and in the revolving heads at the beginning of *Real News for Kids*): How could they have a big fat thing, and then it squeezes in together?
>
> Int: How could they?
>
> Philip: They probably—you know those mirrors when you like, um, there's like a mirror in the shopping mall and then you're like this [demonstrating] and then you squeeze in like this and it's like really thinner and thinner when you go in. It looks really weird.
>
> Int: I see.
>
> Philip: How could they make that world go real fast?

Int: You tell me.

Philip: Well that's probably like a drill or something in a table, but you can't see under the table and she's probably twisting like this.

Int: Wow, yeah. Well who's doing all this stuff then?

Philip: Who makes them up?

Int: Yes.

Philip: Someone like, well, people that organize TV shows.

Int: Do you know who they are?

Philip: No.

Here is fellow first-grader Jack, talking about the same introductory graphics:

Jack: People can't fly sideways and they can't go up and swash their heads. People can't swirl their head around and like have two heads.

Int: How do you think they have done this with these colors?

Jack: Maybe they have done this with a computer—they put pictures that they made.

Int: Why do you think that they would do this?

Jack: Maybe they are going to tell what's going to happen tomorrow.

Int: What do you mean by that?

Jack: Maybe it is like the song in the beginning. Some TV shows always have a part where they begin the show and then they sing the song. They did begin the show and then sing the song and maybe starting the beginning of the song.

Both these first graders identified the unreality of the credit sequence. One used it to make an interesting comparison with his experience of distorting mirrors, making no reference to TV technology at all. The other correctly identified the involvement of computers in how it was done and also correctly identified the sequence as a credit sequence "telling you what's going to happen." These younger children's explanations, as would have been predicted from earlier research, stuck firmly to surface features. Older children were able to widen their frames of contextual reference:

Paul (third grade): They can't like just pop in the screen and have them changed.

Int: Why do you think they use all these colorful things?

Paul: So that people would want to watch it.

Fourth-grade Sarah demonstrated the decreasing salience of special effects as a reality marker for older children, particularly girls, by ignoring the graphics of the credit sequence altogether. She was asked after the sequence whether she had noticed these unrealistic images, and she said she had:

Int: Why did you not press pause?

Sarah: You kind of know that's trick photography. It is not supposed to be real. It's just the beginning of the thing and they usually do things like that.

Int: How do you know it's not supposed to be real?

Sarah: I don't, but usually they just do things like that just to start off the show.

PASSING JUDGMENTS

One of the most thought-provoking findings from the questionnaire stage of the research was in the area of prosocial judgments, that is, the extent to which children, particularly girls, disapproved of the use of television illusion to deceive. The sequences used in the interview sessions provided very little opportunity for children to express moral disapproval along these lines; most of the interviewees, unlike Neil Postman and the Republican Right, approved of *Sesame Street* using cartoons, humor, and Muppets to "educate little kids," although some were anxious to distance themselves from the little-kids category:

Int: Who would watch it?

Ryan (third grade): Like 4 years old.

Int: Would you watch it?

Ryan: Not *Sesame Street*.

Int: What do you think of it?

Ryan: I don't like it.

Int: What would you like?

Ryan: I like movies like fighting.

Some of the older children admitted that they sometimes still watched it, but not Lauren (fourth grade), "because we already know this stuff." Most could see that it was "a good program for younger kids," but were careful to point out that "It's . . . not for older kids" (Elijah, third grade). Their distinctions were made on the basis of the program's use of cartoons, and of fun, as well as on their awareness that they themselves had progressed beyond the show's knowledge level. These children also saw themselves as having progressed beyond the kinds of techniques used in *Sesame Street* and not just the information given in it. (This is ironic because the program is greatly enjoyed by college students and adults for its clever allusiveness.) One child pointed out the difference between it and *Real News for Kids:*

> Tim (fifth grade): The other one [*Sesame Street*] is basically cartoons ... and characters are real in this one [*Real News*].

Ruth (third grade), along with a number of children, expressed her own theories of maturation, drawing a developmental line, as do older theorists on the subject, at around the age of 6 or 7.

> Ruth: Older people don't like watching a lot of little cartoons and young people do.
>
> Int: And when do they change and stop enjoying it?
>
> Ruth: Around 6 or 7.
>
> Int: Why do you think that is?
>
> Ruth: Because then you like watching regular things that aren't cartoons.

Value judgments were, as in this case, based on the appropriateness of the material to its audience, rather than on wider social and moral issues. The show was deemed to be childish, but appropriately so, because of its genre and because of its intended viewers. Similarly, these children could accept the lack of realism in *The Cosby Show*'s depiction of family relationships on the grounds that it was a situation comedy and, therefore, the situations had to be funny rather than strictly naturalistic. (Awareness of humor is a surprising omission from some of the other research literature on the show, from which a nonviewer would never know that it was meant to be—and very often was—extremely funny. Julian Sefton-Green's 1990 interviews are a case in point.) Given *The Sand Fairy*'s perceived status as a fairy tale, this, too, generated no disapproval of its considerable distortions of time, place, and physical laws. As one fourth-grader patiently pointed out in answer to the question, "Why do you think they use these effects"?: "It is *supposed* to be a fairy tale."

However, there was one area of television production that did not escape more moralistic judgmental comment, namely commercials. A number of interviewees showed that they were aware of commercial pressures in programming, for instance, third-grade Elijah, talking about the rapid intercutting from one person to another in *Real News for Kids:*

> Elijah: They couldn't go from all those people that fast.
>
> Int: Why do it that way rather than just do it slowly?

Elijah: Because it wastes some time and they need time for commercials.

Int: Do you think it helps people to understand what's happening?

Elijah: Not really, because most of the important part stays slower.

This is a clear example of how a modality judgment—about editing—can be led into a broader pragmatic judgment about the need for speed to save time for commercials (pragmatic/effects). Then, Elijah explicitly states the importance of formal features in making a judgment about how seriously to take the material: one way of identifying "the important parts" is noticing their slower pace.

Many children had direct experience with the misleading nature of commercials. First-grade Natasha paused the tape at the commercial for the drawing toy, which showed drawings magically and quickly materializing:

Natasha: They're just trying to make it look better.

Int: What are they doing?

Natasha: They're just going over lines, but they're making it go faster. It will go slow when you have it. My grandma got me this thing, and the second time I used it, it broke.

Int: Why are they doing it that way?

Natasha: So that people would buy it.

The most eloquent indictment of the misleading nature of commercials came from fifth-grade Ben, who had "read a lot of stuff in books" about computer animation, and who also had some experience with editing. Ben was an excellent, if rare, example of a child who was able to utilize this knowledge in order to make wider institutional judgments about media production and ethics. (He was the child who commented on the lack of realism in *The Cosby Show*.) He paused the tape at the commercial for the drawing toy:

Ben: I wouldn't believe that would come with all that paper. There must be like five or six sets combined.

Int: Why did they do it?

Ben: They're doing it so people will think that it will cost a lot, but it really doesn't.

Int: What do you think about that?

Ben: It probably cost a dollar to make them and they probably sell it for thirty.

Int: What do you think about that?

Ben: I would not buy it.

[Referring to the next ad, for Swanns Crossing dolls]: Those sets in the background don't come with it. Actually, the kids don't make it. The adults on the crew and maintenance make it. It looks like the kids make it. Actually it doesn't even look like the kids made it. It looks like it comes with the set of dolls itself, but it really doesn't.

Int: Again, what's the point of creating that?

Ben: So it looks more exciting than what it really is. The arms probably don't even move.

Int: So what's going on here?

Ben: They're just trying to get you to buy them. It's like yesterday I was on the bus and these kids, they buy these little toys. Little crummy toys, they're about six bucks, action figures, and they don't even do anything. I mean, like it's one thing if you buy something that's worth your money, like something to invest in, like sports cars, stocks etc. or something like that.

The indignation here is an intriguing mixture of genuine concern about little kids being exploited, and a canny desire to get value for money in the form of stocks and sports cars. Ben showed similar indignation at the deceptions of computer animation, as in the *Real News* graphics:

Ben: It's to make it look cool. In fact, it does look cool, because if it's not real, people might think that's real and think they might get a real education.

Int: Who might think it was real?

Ben: Little kids. Maybe, like, bums who walk into TV stores in New York City. Just anybody might think that it was real and it isn't. It is just a computer. These computers make images on the computer and they can make it, uh, like, uh, PS2. They mostly use IBM.

The accents of Huckleberry Finn, and of Holden Caulfield with his contempt for the phony, and of Lisa Simpson, their modern descendant, can be heard here. Much of adults' moralistic concern about television, in contrast, is not about phoniness, but about violence, which many children quite like, such as Ryan, already quoted. The questionnaire evidence suggests, too, that boys especially do not object to the use of exaggerated violence "to make stories more exciting". The children's comments demonstrated a protectiveness on the part of older children for younger ones, however, and there is evidence that children, like adults, believe that watching violence is all right for them, but they disapprove of it for children younger than themselves (Davies, 1990).

Ben's eloquence on the subject of being conned, of people being sold inferior products when they could be getting "a real education," suggests that moralistic approaches to the media might be more inspiring to children if issues of deceit and deception, of the legitimate versus the nonlegitimate distortion of reality, were presented as key moral issues. Such issues may well have more salience for the young than abstract questions about fantasy violence, which for many children (sadly, not all), has no bearing on their everyday lives. For those for whom violence *is* an everyday reality, the question of its representation in the media becomes very much a question of whether this representation is deceptive or whether it serves the needs of victimized children by dealing with the subject truthfully, from their perspective. As with other areas of representation, the moral issue is not about the setting of bad examples, but of what is the truth, and what versions of the truth are most helpful to children at different stages of their development. Ben's comments raise again the issue of truth versus realism, and Bettelheim's (1976) and Lurie's (1990) arguments about the sometimes brutal truthfulness of fairy-tale fiction versus the well-meaning but anodyne deceptions of "relevant" realism. They also underline the point that emerged from children's responses to the *Real News for Kids* item: that fancy televisual packaging intended to make complex ideas relevant to children, can get in the way of meaning rather than enhance it. To Ben at least, a highly literate viewer, these kinds of deceptions are to be deplored.

12

"Charming Our Leisure": Why Media Matter

In his review of media education programs around the world, Brown (1993) summarized the three main approaches that he identified in these programs:

1. Inoculation: teaching children about the media in order to arm them against harmful effects, which Brown described as moralistic.
2. Critical viewing: teaching children about formal features in ways that Brown calls "increasingly pluralistic, non-directive, and non-value-laden."
3. Community media approaches: These last, according to Brown, have grown out of "desperate social and economic contexts, with strong valuative judgments directed against mass media empires." (p. 322)

Brown proposed "a menu of possible agendas for the next wave of educators who realize anew the significant link between television viewing and social, aesthetic, economic reality, as well as specific learning skills" (p. 322) .

This menu included four main groups of recommendations:

1. Administrative support
2. The training of teachers
3. The development of holistic, integrated critical-viewing skills curricula (Brown warns against reinventing the wheel and points out the existence of much useful material from earlier projects)
4. The involvement of parents and the home

There is a significant omission from this list—an omission that has been the subject of this book. This omission is children themselves. Without an understanding of how children themselves relate to mass media experience, how they interpret it, teach themselves about it, relate it to other experiences in their lives; how they talk, speculate, think, and hypothesize about it, none of these other initiatives is complete. Media education is different from other education and virtually unique as a subject area because many of the pupils are likely to have more direct experience as consumers of the products under review than have their teachers.

Media education does not involve introducing completely unfamiliar subject matter and learning procedures in the way that mathematics, foreign language, or computer programming do. When most children come into school full time, at 5 in the United Kingdom, and 6 in the United States, they have already listened to and watched hundreds of stories, sung along with thousands of songs and jingles, been exposed to thousands of commercials and hundreds of thousands of images, many depicting unfamiliar areas of experience, such as war or the legal system, or for city children, the countryside, and for rural children, big cities. They have seen huge advertising posters as they have been pushed along in their strollers; they have heard rock, classical, country, and jazz music on the radio, on disc, or on cassette—their own or other people's; they have overheard news bulletins and played with (no doubt, to their parents' annoyance) newspapers and magazines as they sat in their playpens. Many of them will have learned to find their way around computer screens. This study has been an attempt to answer the question: What do they make of this?

The sample of children used in the study, particularly in the interview section, were a useful sample in helping to answer this question because they had never received any formal media education. In other respects, they seemed to have every advantage; they were prosperous, attending good schools, bright, happy, healthy, and friendly, as one would want all children to be. The information they offered about their views on television reality and their theories about how and why the medium was unreal came, therefore, from their own experience, (which, of course, included their schooling) and their own reflections on their experiences. Whatever the views they expressed—as illustrated in the samples given in this book—and however idiosyncratic, reflective, discerning, or incomplete these views were—these views were their own. They had been formed in the interstices of their home and school lives, perhaps through solitary reflection, perhaps through discussions with siblings, with peers, or through playground fantasy games, perhaps through conversations with grown-ups, and certainly through reading, TV viewing and film going. A major source of their information about how media work was the media themselves; when asked how they knew about "green screens" or "clay animation," the children would mention seeing it on a TV show or reading about it in a book, or, in some cases, through visits to Disneyland. Sometimes, they did not know where the information had come from. They "just knew it."

Any new initiatives to promote education about the media for children in this age group must recognize the fertile subsoils of knowledge and mental theorizing on media issues that children bring into school with them and with which their teachers will have to work. Young children are not, nor have they ever been blank slates—even at birth. But 5- and 6-year-old children in Britain, the United States, and other developed countries, are especially not blank slates when it comes to experiences of, and theories about, the workings of mass media. This study has been an attempt to demonstrate that.

THE VALUE OF TALK

At the end of chapter 2 of Jane Austen's *Mansfield Park* is an excellent definition of both the value of leisure, and the value of talk in humanistic education. Referring to the way in which 10-year-old Fanny Price is protected and encouraged by her older cousin Edmund, Austen wrote:

> He recommended the books which charmed her leisure hours, he encouraged her taste and corrected her judgment; *he made reading useful by talking to her of what she read,* and heightened its attraction by judicious praise. (Oxford paperback edition, 1990, p.19) [my emphases]

As already discussed in chapter 6, there are drawbacks to relying on talk data for the purposes of research. But using talk in education for the purpose of making reading and leisure useful, and the importance of praise rather than censure in heightening the attractions of learning, are sound pedagogic procedures. We know how well they worked for Jane Austen, not only from her books, which are filled with lively and instructive dialogue, some of it about media such as books, poetry, music, and theater, but also from her own and other people's letters and journals. Talk as a way of making reading useful is a metacognitive process, requiring readers to reflect on their own thoughts and to analyze their own experiences. Reading is not useful, as Austen suggests, unless reflected on.

One of the advantages of the interview procedure used in this study was the opportunity it gave for these children to talk and reflect. All the children, with the exception of one first-grade girl, who was not feeling well, were uninhibited, and many enthusiastically seized the opportunity to discuss their ideas and knowledge about the medium. I hope that the transcripts give a flavor of the intellectual processes that were going on as the children talked; it was certainly clear to me, as one of the interviewers, that these children accepted that they were being treated in an adult way, as partners in discovery, and they used the opportunity accordingly to reflect, theorize, debate, and articulate their ideas.

Strange interviewers are not the ideal partners in talk, because children may be shy. On the other hand, strangers are useful in research because they can sometimes elicit more information than familiar teachers and parents can by being naive questioners. The children know that the interviewer knows nothing about them, and hence the questions seem reasonable. This is not the case with a parent who asks, "What is your favorite television program?" The child knows that the parent knows perfectly well. I am not proposing that an interview strategy should be used as a routine pedagogic technique—although getting children to conduct their own research project with the help of adults could be one way of generating similarly productive talk sessions in the classroom. But I would argue from my experience with this study that ways need to be found within the classroom for children to theorize, speculate, analyze, reflect, and make judgments on aspects of mass media that may some-times be taken for granted—such as popular situation comedies, children's cartoons, commercials, or news bulletins.

These learning situations need to be open-ended rather than prescrip-tive because, hard though it is for us grown-ups to accept, adults do not necessarily always know best about the media and their representations. Adults do not have all the critical-viewing skills at their fingertips, any more than children do. They may also have their own agendas, to use an overworked word, about the children they are dealing with—about their class, sex, race, religion, intelligence level, and so on, and about how children with different backgrounds are supposed to behave and think. Fortunately for the future of the human race and its continuing evolution, children do not always know how they are supposed to behave and think. Even when they do, they still often refuse to conform to expectations (as parents find out). Adults need to be prepared to listen to children as well as to instruct. Hence, there needs to be a space for open-ended inquiry in all critical-viewing-skills curricula.

THE CHARM OF LEISURE HOURS

Fanny Price's love of reading in her leisure hours would be smiled on by most adults today, and seen as an essential component of a good educa-tion. (It was not always so, even in my childhood, when I was regularly scolded for having my nose perpetually stuck in a book.) Austen's use of the words *charm, attraction, judicious praise* all indicate the importance that she attached to pleasure in the consumption of literary material. In this case, the pleasure is higher even than the pleasure of reading; it is a form of passionate seduction, at least for Fanny, who falls in love with Edmund as a result of his encouragement: "In return for such services she loved him better than anybody in the world." (p. 19)

It is easy for educators to look back at such an era with nostalgia; if only children now would fall in love over books. We forget that in every age, the consumption of fiction for leisure has had its moralistic critics (see Starker, 1991). Ironically, Jane Austen herself—although satirizing excessive indulgence in fictional fantasy in *Northanger Abbey*, published in 1817—provided one of the most spirited defenses of fiction's proper use in the same book:

> Although our productions have afforded more extensive and unaffected pleasure than those of any other literary corporation in the world, no species of composition has been so much decried. . . ."Do not imagine that *I* often read novels" . . . Such is the common cant. . . . "Oh it is only a novel" . . . in short, only some work in which the greatest powers of the mind are displayed, in which the most thorough knowledge of human nature, the happiest delineation of its varieties, the liveliest effusions of wit and humour are conveyed to the world in the best chosen language. (p. 34)

Somewhat different priorities are found in the writings of media educators. Brown (1993) concluded his discussion of critical-viewing-skills programs by summarizing what teachers and administrators need to do to put together coherent media-education curricula:

> They must select from paradigmatic projects the extent to which they want to study mass media as texts, to be read and deconstructed and demystified and demythologized, as semiotic phenomena (with connotation, repre-sentation, and ideology) and as industries (including ownership and con-trol).
>
> [T]he larger social and economic and political aspects of the medium must be explored.
>
> [C]ritical viewing skills training should not be limited to "visual literacy".
>
> [V]iewers should not only enhance their appreciation of media product, but also grow in realization of "mediation" in society, which is a function of the traditions, ideals, myths, and established forces (business, government, socioeconomic ideology itself) driving that society and its values. (pp. 325–326)

This is an admirable summary, but how different is this way of talking about the media (the repeated use of the term viewer suggests that Brown is only talking about television) to Jane Austen's on the subject of books. No mention of leisure, or of charm, attraction, praise, or love here; nothing about pleasure or liveliness or humor. Yet books are mass media, too, and if Brown's recommendations are valid, there seems no logical reason why children in English literature classes should not also scrutinize the proc-esses of production, the publishing empires, the cultural specificity, the history, economics, politics, and institutional practices of the publishing industry, including the thriving academic branches of it, so beholden to Austen's "injured body" of creative writers.

The answer, I hope, of any school teacher of English to this suggestion would be that there is no point in teaching children about the publishing industry until they first have an understanding, an appreciation, a knowledge, and hopefully a love of books: of stories, plays, poems, picture books, text books, pop-up cartoon books, cloth books, second-hand books, and pristine new books. When they know and care about books, then questions about hegemony in the publishing industry will matter to them. But if books are not important, then why should anyone, least of all an 8-year-old, care about the publishing industry?

The same answer can be made about television. There is no point in teaching children about the merger between ABC and Disney if they have never been given an opportunity to talk about *The Lion King* or *Beauty and the Beast*. If shows like *Full House* and *Sesame Street,* or *Five Children and It, Blue Peter* or *Neighbours* charm their leisure hours, then the importance of the pleasure that children take in these stories must be recognized. If we want them to appreciate more demanding screen material like *Nova* or *Middlemarch,* or foreign-language movies (not to mention the books on which these are so often based), we have to recognize the importance of enjoyment in leading children toward more demanding cultural experiences. This is a point made well by Susan Neumann in her review of the not always negative relationship between television and reading (Neumann, 1986).

DEVELOPMENTAL IMPLICATIONS

A further reason for grounding media and cultural education for this age group in personal experience is a developmental one. As this and other studies suggest, young children only gradually acquire the complex mental schemata of metacognition and metarepresentation over time. The mental networks of information formed from real-world knowledge, plus the increasingly complex logical, symbolic, and linguistic abilities needed to transform and apply this knowledge to mediated representations, take years to be built up. The acquisition of these abilities, as with other skills, is through the twofold and interacting processes of maturation and practice—nature and nurture, biological development, plus education in its widest sense, including both leisure and classroom activities.

In dealing with mediated representations, children roughly below the age of 8 (although there are always more mature exceptions) tend to focus on the immediate, the concrete, the personal, and the idiosyncratic. Their interpretations are often very charming to adults—for instance, Big Bird being unreal because he is too big to sit on a piano stool—but they are serious and meaningful to children and need to be taken seriously by us, rather than rationally deconstructed or corrected. Such young children have a world-view that still has room for the impossible: for a future with "real good magic things," for a past where fantasy castles were more likely than they are now, and for a present that still includes Santa Claus. Older children, as this study demonstrated, recognize the importance of magic, including the special magic of television techniques and effects, for the little kids in the *Sesame Street* audience, but emphatically not for themselves. This finding of the study suggests a marked developmental shift towards rationalism at around the age of 7 or 8, a period also identified by theorists such as Piaget and Howard Gardner as critical in intellectual and linguistic progress. The likely connection between these developments is underlined by the shift in children's media tastes at this age away from fantasy and cartoons and toward realistic representations, comedy, and real-world events such as sports.

SOCIAL AWARENESS

Awareness of real world probability and concomitant judgments about media plausibility plus awareness of context and pragmatic inferences about other people's points of view, become more prevalent and practiced as children get older. On the threshold of adolescence, children become less interested in the formal trappings of media products and begin to be aware of the importance of representing reality realistically, thereby raising social, institutional, and political implications. In the questionnaire stage of my study, there was a striking difference between boys and girls on the ethics of media deception, with girls more strongly disapproving of such deceptions. The girls were also less interested in the technicalities of the medium than were boys. This is a difference that is worth exploring with children from other backgrounds. Only one interviewee in the study—11-year-old Ben—was able to articulate sociopolitical perspectives with any clarity. Nevertheless, such ways of thinking should certainly be within the intellectual reach of children starting secondary school or junior high school.

THE USES OF SUBVERSION

Perhaps if Ben and his peers had been receiving media education, more of the children in the study would have demonstrated sociopolitical awareness, perhaps not. I suspect that however much we try to influence preadolescent children with politically or morally acceptable agendas, developmental constraints will necessarily—and healthily—limit their being completely assimilated. I agree with Alison Lurie (1990), although I believe that more empirical evidence is needed: preadolescent childrens readings of different kinds of media texts, particularly adult-approved ones, are likely to be oppositional. Lurie called children's literature "subversive," because "its values are not always those of the conventional adult world." (p. xi) She argued that the best children's literature offers "other views of human life besides those of the shopping mall and the corporation." (p. xi) It also offers other views besides the liberal, the conservative, the virtuous, or the politically correct. According to Lurie

> If by chance we should want to know what has been censored from establishment culture in the past, or what our kids are really up to today, we might do well to look at the classic children's books and listen to the rhymes being sung on school playgrounds. (Lurie, 1990, p. 15)

This raises what Hodge and Tripp (1986) called "the continuing political dimension" of reality and modality judgments (p. 101). My own view is that children's tendency to resist adult-imposed ideologies and behaviors through their private rituals, games, fantasies, tastes, and interpretations of reality, both in life and in art, is a developmentally desirable one, and it has the evolutionary survival value of making sure that human diversity and adaptability continue. Children's abiding pre-occupation with alternative realities—with pretend games—almost from birth, suggests an extreme unwillingness to accept, untested, adult versions of what life is supposed to be about. To put it more bluntly, kids are hard to brainwash. However, the question of whether children naturally or otherwise can develop raised political consciousness about media representations can only be tested with a much larger and more socially representative sample than mine.

THE IMPORTANCE OF PLEASURE

Entertainment—the main reason given by most TV viewers for watching the medium—has rarely been seen as a legitimate educational goal. The irony in the title of Richard Dyer's celebratory book on the subject, *"Only* (my emphasis) *Entertainment"* (Dyer, 1992), assumes a general belief about the low pedagogic value of having a good time. As Dyer pointed out, (in his case, with a special emphasis on gay culture, but the culture of childhood belongs in a similar oppositional category), pleasure, too, has a political dimension. The omission of enjoyment from Brown's otherwise comprehensive summary of the necessary ingredients of media-education programs means that, from the viewer/reader's perspective, these educational programs are built around a vacuum. There is an empty space where a consideration of the kinds of direct experience enjoyed by Fanny Price and Edmund Bertram in *Mansfield Park* should be. Such pleasurable experiences, even when shared, are always ultimately at the individual level, and as such, they are potentially subversive, as Austen illustrates through Fanny's obdurate, but private resistance to a range of powerful social pressures. Fanny's unnoticed resistance to the values of the corrupted world around her, supported by her "useful and charming" leisure reading, is vindicated by the triumphant (for her) conclusion of the novel, in contrast to the "guilt and misery" of those who failed to resist these values. She is an unusual heroine and, to many, an unattractive one, but in drawing her strength from private emotion and reflection, she is certainly not an implausible one.

The consumption of television, too, paradoxically, is a private and domestic activity, even though it is produced by factorylike processes, and reaches huge numbers of people. Indeed, television-viewing has received some of its fiercest criticism precisely because it appears to cut individuals off from the social world. Winn (1985) lamented, in *The Plug-In Drug*, that children watching TV appear to be lost in a private world, oblivious to everything around them. (So of course, do children reading books, an even more private, because exclusive, activity.) The fact remains that, whether we are receiving information as members of a large public audience, or a small domestic one, or completely on our own, the processing of any given media message, image, or story can only be experienced at the level of individual consciousness. Meaning happens in minds—or, to be strictly physiologically accurate, in brains and nervous systems—not in factories and certainly not in masses which, as Williams (1974) wisely pointed out, do not exist except as a way of talking. (See also Ang's excellent discussion of the ways in which mass audiences are invented and reified in her 1991 book *Desperately Seeking the Audience.*)

It is only because individuals like, enjoy and are charmed by the cultural products of TV, film, and mass publishing that they matter at all. The fact that, when a lot of individuals' tastes are added together, the result is a mass audience, is not a factor in the quality of the individual experience. Like other shared experiences, it may be discussed with friends, family, colleagues, and, perhaps, through fan groups. However, audiences cannot identify themselves as a *mass*. Indeed, my informal research with groups of audiences has shown that they find it almost impossible to define the term. Conceiving of groups consisting of millions, or thousands of people is difficult for adults, and virtually impossible for children. Watching TV, as with reading a book, is a personal experience. This is not just a well-meaning liberal statement. It is also a commercial truism. Audiences are the commodity that is bought and sold in the media business. Audiences, however, have their own agendas. When people like or even love something, even if other people think it is not very good for them, no amount of educational theorizing is going to make them stop liking it; the (highly subversive) plot of *Mansfield Park* is as good an illustration of this principle as can be found. Children like television, and they like other media too, including books. Individual children's tastes vary quite a lot (see the data in chapter 5). Often the same children who like books also like television and film—another finding of Susan Neumann's 1986 study. Media educators need to work with this grain, not against it. Whether television, film, and books are always worthy of their love is another question.

THE QUALITY OF MEDIA TEXTS

In Britain, so far (though times are changing), many would argue that television has often been worthy of the devotion of its audiences. Television has been a fascinatingly creative, vibrant, socially important medium in which, according to critic and screenwriter Andrew Davies, nearly all the best dramatic writing of the last 25 years has been done (Davies, 1994). Some of this writing has been done for children, too. In the more intensely commercial broadcasting system of the United States, creative writers and producers have had to be more ingenious—and subversive. Excellence and creativity are smuggled out to the public via standard commercial formats, as in *Roseanne*, *The Cosby Show*, and *Cheers*, and in the fierce Swiftian satire of *The Simpsons*, posing innocently, like Gulliver, as a children's fable. Occasionally, excellence and creativity present themselves without disguise, as in Barry Levinson's majestic *Homicide—Life on the Streets*. But I suspect that any academic who wanted to pay the same kind of serious critical attention to *Cheers* or to *Homicide* as is given to a novelist like Jane Austen would be deemed a little eccentric.

The people who write, direct, design, and produce the texts that charm our leisure hours nowadays are worthy of critical attention, because it is only through informed and serious critical attention that good work can be encouraged and mediocre work improved, and it is a fundamental goal of pedagogy to generate good work. The quality of the individual (and diverse) achievements of Bill Cosby, Matt Groening, Steven Bochco, and Roseanne, and the designers, teachers, and producers at the Children's Television Workshop, therefore, matters; the caliber of the students who enter the creative media fields (like those I teach) matters; and the quality of the critical attention given to their work by the students of tomorrow—like the children I interviewed—matters, too. These children were in no doubt that behind the effects and performances they were observing were people: writers, producers, "the guy on the camera," "somebody in a costume," actors. Some of them also had a strong sense that these people should be held to account for the ways in which they deceived or exploited their audiences, particularly other "little kids."

It is easy for the intellectually privileged to be pessimistic about mass-produced culture—the vulgar and trashy "carnival culture" of 20th century America, in James Twitchell's (1993) words, as if there were something self-evidently wrong with carnivals (or indeed, with being vulgar). It is easy to condemn popular culture out of hand as violent, commercial, and debasing, or to argue that the process of mass production has destroyed all meaningful standards of cultural evaluation, and then to retreat to the opera. Even the defenders of popular culture may defend it in such terms as to patronize it, proposing that there are no accepted standards of cultural evaluation any more because judgments about standards are elitist and outmoded.

This is selling the pass—a contemporary *trahison des clercs*. Such assumptions are also antieducational; those of my colleagues who teach film and video production, journalism, photography, screen-writing, and design, and their students, know well that without high and demanding standards of performance, their efforts are meaningless and the ideas that they want to convey to their audiences will be lost. The same is true of those of us who teach theoretical subjects, who also need to place high expectations of performance on students. Despite an inevitable degree of subjectivity in assessments, an A-grade essay is always better than a D-grade essay, and the students know it. They do not want us to tell them that a D is as good as an A. They want us to teach them how to improve from D to A. Criteria of performance are always necessary and should be as explicit as possible if students are to learn effectively. The kinds of modality judgments made by the children in my study, about what is being said, and how, and by whom, and to what end, are the basis of such criteria. They are also an essential part of being a critical citizen in the mediated world in which we live.

ART EXPRESSES LIFE

Teachers of creative students become aware of the truth that emerged from my conversations with the subjects of my study: judgments about the reality and credibility of media representations are often inseparable from evaluative judgments about the forms in which they are constructed. Art expresses life, and the more effective the art, the more effective the expression. Such teachers and students also know that, despite being part of a huge and technologically sophisticated industry, what they are doing can still be called art.

The quality of the broadcast media in the United States, in Britain, and everywhere (but particularly in the United States, with its almost total dominance of the world media market) is something that media educators should be addressing seriously. It is time to stop attacking the media, particularly the media of film and television, and start making them better, because they are definitely not going to go away. We need to pay attention to and honor what is already good. Mass media will only have a chance to improve their cultural standards, however defined, and their usefulness to the young, when sound critical, professional, and scholarly criteria for excellence and creativity in the popular arts are established. I would like to think that this is beginning to happen through work like Susan Neumann's, through critical studies like those published in Van den Berg and Wenner's (1991) collection, through populist texts such as Bianculli's book on tele-literacy, through the increasing expansion of cultural studies with its close attention to media texts rather than to media effects, and through the continuing and underappreciated efforts of production teachers (see Blanchard & Christ, 1993). These efforts are also being carried on in elementary and high schools where media education programs have been instituted. (See, for example, BFI, Working Papers 1–4, 1986–1988.) Nevertheless, experiences like the one I had of being nearly physically attacked by an eminent literary person in Boston who had heard that I had written a book saying that television was good for kids, may not bode well for the prospects of rational debate.

My much happier experience with the schoolchildren of Philadelphia suggests that the basis for setting up sound critical criteria already exists. If the quality of American broadcasting and mass media is to be improved and sustained, what better place to start than in the elementary-school classroom?

References

Alvarado, M., Gutch, R., & Wollen, T. (1987). *Learning the media: An introduction to media teaching.* London: Macmillan.

Anderson, J. (1990). *Constitutions of the audience in research and theory: Implications for media literacy programs.* Paper given to IVLA Symposium, Verbo-Visual Literacy: Mapping the Field, London, July, 1990.

Ang, I. (1991). *Desperately seeking the audience.* London: Routledge.

Austen, J. (1814, 1991) *Mansfield Park.* London: Penguin.

Austen, J. (1817, 1995). *Northanger Abbey.* London: Penguin.

Bartlett, F. C. (1932). *Remembering.* Cambridge: Cambridge University Press.

Bazalgette, C. (1991). *Teaching English in the National Curriculum: Media Education*, London: Hodder & Stoughton.

Bazalgette, C. (Ed.) (1988). *Primary Media Education.* London: British Film Institute.

Bettelheim, B. (1976). *The Uses Of Enchantment,* London: Thames & Hudson.

Bianculli, D. (1992). *Tele-literacy: Taking television seriously.* New York: Continuum.

Blanchard, R. & Christ, W. (1993). *Media education and the liberal arts.* Hillsdale, NJ: Lawrence Erlbaum Associates.

Bourdieu, P. (1984). *Distinction: A social critique of the judgement of taste.* Cambridge, MA: Harvard University Press.

British Film Institute (1986-1988). *Working papers 1, 2, 3, 4,* London: British Film Institute.

British Film Institute, (1988). *Primary Media Education.* London: British Film Institute.

Brown, J. A. (1993). *Television "critical viewing skills" education: major media literacy projects in the United States and selected countries.* Hillsdale NJ: Lawrence Erlbaum Associates.

Bruner, J. (1986). *Actual minds, possible worlds.* Cambridge, MA: Harvard University Press.

Buckingham, D. (1988). *Television literacy: a critique,* Paper presented to the International Television Studies Conference, Institute of Education, University of London.

Buckingham, D. (1993a). *Children talking television: The making of television literacy.* London: Falmer Press.

Buckingham, D. (1993b), *Reading audiences: Young people and the media.* Manchester: Manchester University Press.

Cantor, J. (1994). Confronting children's fright responses to media. In Zillmann, D., Bent, J., & Huston, A. C. (Eds.), *Media, Children and the family: Social scientific, psychodynamic and clinical perspectives* Hillsdale, NJ: Lawrence Erlbaum Associates.

Carroll, J. M. (1980). *Towards a structural psychology of the cinema,* The Hague: Mouton.

Davies, A. (1994). *Prima donnas and job lots.* Huw Weldon Memorial Lecture, Royal Television Society, London: December 1994.

Davies, M. M., Lloyd, E., & Scheffler, A. (1987). *Baby language.* London: Unwin Hyman.

Davies, M. M. (1988). *An investigation into certain effects of television camera techniques on cognitive processing.* Unpublished doctoral dissertation, University of East London.

Davies, M. M. (1989). *Television is good for your kids,* London: Hilary Shipman.

Davies, M. M. (1990). *Teenagers' attitudes to violence on TV.* Paper presented to Growing Too Fast, conference organized by British Action for Children's Television and the Broadcasting Standards Council, Royal Society of Arts, London, July 1990.

Davies, M. M. (1995). Babes n the Hood: Preschool television in the USA and Britain. In Bazalgette, C. & Buckingham, D. (Eds.) *In front of the children: Screen entertainment and young audiences.* London: British Film Institute.

Davies, M. M. (1996). Making media literate: Educating future media workers at undergraduate level. In R. Kubey and B. Ruben (Eds.), *Literacy in the information age: Information & behavior, Vol. 6,* New Brunswick, NJ: Transaction.

Dent, C., & Rosenberg, L. (1990). Developmental accounts of children's processing of non-literal material, visual and verbal metaphors: developmental interactions. *Child Development, 61,* 983–984.

Dorr, A. (1983). No shortcuts to judging reality. In J. Bent & D. Anderson (Eds.), *Children's understanding of television.* New York: Academic Press.

Dorr, A., Kovaric, P., & Doubleday, C. (1990). Age and content influences on children's perceptions of the realism of television families, *Journal of Broadcasting & Educational Media, 34,* (4) 377–397.

Dyer, R. (1992). *Only entertainment.* London: Routledge.

Eisenberg, N. & Mussen, P. H. (1989). *The roots of prosocial behavior in children.* Cambridge: Cambridge University Press.

Eisenstein, S. (1943). *The film sense.* (J. Leyda, Trans.). London: Faber & Faber.

Eke, R. & Croll, P. (1992). Television formats and children's classification of their viewing, *Journal of Educational Television, 18* (2–3), 97–105.

Elliott, W. (1983). *Measuring the perceived reality of television: perceived plausibility, perceived superficiality and the degree of personal utility.* Paper presented at the annual meeting of the Association for Education in Journalism and Mass Communication, Corvallis, OR, August 6-9, 1983.

Fish, S. (1980). *Is there a text in this class? The authority of interpretive communities.* Harvard University Press: Cambridge, MA.

Gardner, H. (1991). *The unschooled mind: How children think and how schools should teach,* New York: Basic Books.

Gerbner, G., Gross, L., Morgan, M., & Signorielli, N., (1980). Cultural Indicators: Violence Profile No. 11, *Journal Of Communication, 30*(3), 10–29.

Gettas, G. (1992). The globalization of *Sesame Street*: A producer's perspective. *Educational Technology, Research and Development, 38*(4) 55–63.

Gitlin, T. (1983). *Inside prime time.* New York: Pantheon.

Harris, P. L., Brown, E., Marriott, C., Whittall, S., & Harmer, S. (1991). Monsters, ghosts and witches: testing the limits of fantasy-reality distinction in young children. *British Journal of Developmental Psychology, 9,* 105–123.

Hartley, J. (1992). *Tele-ology.* London: Routledge.

Hawkins, R. (1977). The dimensional structure of children's perceptions of TV reality *Communication Research, 4*(3).

Hodge, B. & Tripp, D. (1986). *Children and television.* Cambridge: Polity Press.

Jamieson, K. (1993). *Dirty politics: deception, distraction and democracy.* New York: Oxford University Press.

Johnson, J. & Pascual-Leone, J. (1989). Developmental levels of processing in metaphor interpretation. *Journal of Experimental Psychology, 48,* 1–31.

Katz, N., Baker, E., & McNamara J. (1974). What's in a name? A study of how children learn common and proper nouns. *Child Development, 65.*

Kinder, M. (1991). *Playing with power in movies, television and video games from Muppet Babies to Teenage Mutant Ninja Turtles.* Berkeley: University of California Press.

Kraft, R. (1986). The role of cutting in the evaluation and retention of film, *Journal of Experimental Psychology: Learning, Memory and Cognition, 12*, (1), 155–163.

Krasny Brown, L. (1986). *Taking advantage of media: a manual for parents and teachers.* London: Routledge & Kegan Paul.

Kubey, R. & Csickzentmihalyi, M. (1990). *Television and the quality of life: how viewing shapes everyday experience.* Hillsdale, NJ: Lawrence Erlbaum Associates.

Lahr, J. (1995, July 17). Dealing with Roseanne, *The New Yorker,* 42–61.

Laurillard, D. (1993). Balancing the Media, *Journal of Educational Television, 19*, (2), 81–93.

Lenneberg, E. (1967). *Biological foundations of language.* New York: Wiley.

Lesser, G. (1974). *Children and television: Lessons from Sesame Street.* New York: Random House.

Liebes, T., & Katz, E. (1990). *The export of meaning: Cross-cultural readings of Dallas.* New York: Oxford University Press.

Loftus, E. F., & Palmer, J. C. (1974). Reconstruction of automobile destruction: An example of the interaction between language and memory. *Journal of Verbal Learning and Verbal Behavior 13*, 585–589.

Lovelace, V., Scheiner, S., Dollberg, S., Segui, I., & Black, T. (1994). Making a neighborhood the *Sesame Street* way: Developing a methodology to evaluate children's understanding of race. *Journal of Educational Television, 20* (2), 69–78.

Lurie, A. (1990). *Don't tell the grownups: Subversive children's literature.* London: Bloomsbury.

Marshment, M. (1993). The picture is political: Representation of women in contemporary popular culture. In D. Richardson & V. Robinson (Eds.), *An introduction to women's studies.* Basingstoke, England: McMillan.

Messaris, P. (1994). *Visual literacy: Image, mind and reality.* Boulder, CO: Westview Press.

Metz, C. (1974). *Film language: A semiotics of the cinema.* New York: Oxford University Press.

Moore, C., & Frye, D. (1991). The acquisition and utility of theories of mind. In D. Frye & C. Moore (Eds.), *Children's theories of mind: Mental states and social understanding.* Hillsdale, NJ: Lawrence Erlbaum Associates.

Morison, P., Kelly, H., & Gardner, H. (1981). Reasoning about the realities on television: A developmental study. *Journal of Broadcasting, 25* (3), 229–242.

Murphy, C., & Wood, D. J. (1983). Learning through media: A comparison of four to eight year old children's responses to filmed and pictorial instruction. *International Journal of Behavioral Development, 5*, 195–216.

Nesbit, E. (1902) *Five children and It.* London: T. Fisher Unwin.

Neumann, S. B. (1991).*Literacy in the television age.* Norwood, NJ: Ablex.

Neumann, S. B. (1986, July). *Television and reading: A research synthesis.* Paper given to the International Television Studies Conference, Institute of Education, London University.

Newell, A. (1995). Media commentary. *Journal of Educational Television, 21*, (3).

Nikken, P., & Peeters, A. L. (1988). Childrens perceptions of television reality. *Journal of Broadcasting & Electronic Media, 32* (4).

Ochs, E. (1979). *Developmental pragmatics.* New York: Academic Press.

Opie, I., & Opie, P. (1959). *The lore and language of schoolchildren.* Oxford: Oxford University Press.

Palmer, P. (1986a, July), *The social nature of children's television viewing.* Paper presented at the International Television Studies Conference, University of London.

Palmer, P. (1986b). *The lively audience.* Sydney: Unwin Hymen.

Palmer, E. (1988). *Television and America's children: A crisis of neglect.* Oxford: Oxford University Press

Piaget, J., & Inhelder, B. (1968). *The psychology of the child.* New York: Basic Books.

Postman, N. (1985). *The disappearance of childhood.* London: W. H. Allen.

Potter, W. J. (1988). Perceived reality in television effects research. *Journal of Broadcasting & Electronic Media, 32* (1) 32–41.

Real, M. (1991). Bill Cosby and recoding ethnicity. In L. R. Van de Berg & L. Wenner (Eds.), *TV criticism: Approaches and applications.* New York: Longman.

Richards, M. P. M. (1974). *The integration of a child into a social world.* Cambridge: Cambridge University Press.

Richards, M. P. M., & Light, P. (1986). *Children of social worlds.* Cambridge: Polity Press.

Rice, M. L., Huston, A. C., & Wright, J. C. (1983). The forms of television: Effects on children's attention, comprehension and social behavior. In M. Meyer (Ed.), *Children and the formal features of television: Approaches and findings of experimental and formative research.* Munich: K. G. Saur.

Salomon, G. (1977). Effects of encouraging Israeli mothers to co-observe *Sesame Street* with their children. *Child Development, 48* (3) 1146–1151.

Salomon, G. (1979). *Interaction of media, cognition and learning.* San Francisco: Jossey Bass.

Samuels, A., & Taylor, M. (1994). Children's ability to distinguish fantasy events from real-life events. *British Journal of Developmental Psychology, 12* (4), 417–427.

Sefton-Green, J. (1990). Culture and *The Cosby Show.* In D. Buckingham (Ed.), *Watching media learning.* Basingstoke: Falmer Press.

Singer, J., & Singer, D. (1976). Can TV stimulate imaginative play? *Journal of Communication, 26,* 74–80.

Sparks, G., & Cantor, J. (1986). Developmental differences in fright responses to a television program depicting a character transformation. *Journal of Broadcasting and Electronic Media, 30,* 309–323.

Starker, S. (1991). *Evil influences: Crusades against the mass media,* New Brunswick, NJ: Transaction.

Twitchell, J. (1993). *Carnival culture: The trashing of taste in America.* New York: Columbia University Press.

Van de Berg, L. R., & Wenner, L. (Eds.) (1991). *TV criticism: Approaches and applications.* New York: Longman.

Viglietta, L. (1992). Making a science education video: a teacher trainer's perspective, *Journal of Educational Television, 18* (2–3), 117–127.

Watson, R. (1990). *Film and television in education: An aesthetic approach to the moving image.* Basingstoke, England: Falmer Press.

Williams, R. (1974). *Television, technology and cultural form.* London: Fontana/Collins.

Wimmer, R. D., & Dominick, J. R. (1991). *Mass media research: An introduction.* Belmont, CA: Wadsworth.

Winn, M. (1985). *The plug-in drug.* Harmondsworth, England: Penguin.

Wober, M., & Gunter, B. (1986). *Television and social control.* Aldershot, UK: Avebury.

Young, B. (1984). *New approaches to old problems: The growth of advertising literacy.* Conference on international perspectives on TV advertising and children, Mallemort en Provence.

Appendix A

Questionnaire for First and Second Graders

TV Research

Name

Age

School

Grade

Do you have a video recorder at home?

YES

NO

Do you have a video camera at home?

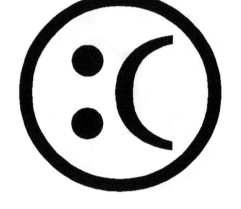

YES   NO

Have you ever programmed a VCR?

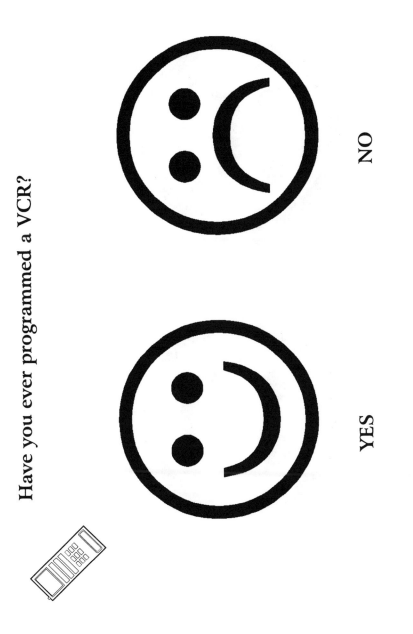

YES

NO

Have you ever used a video camera?

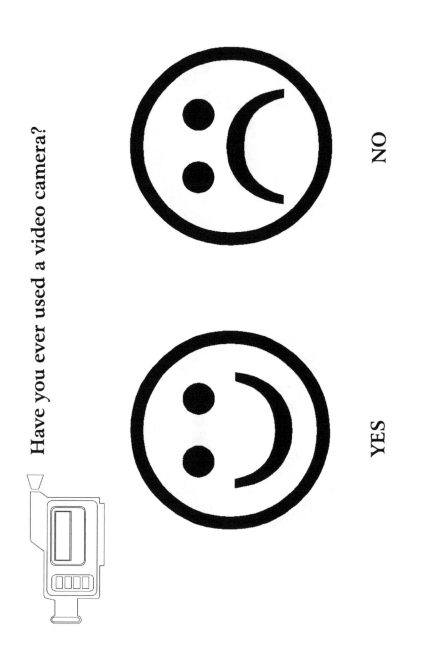

YES   NO

Does anyone in your house work with television or radio or film?

YES   NO

I watch TV:

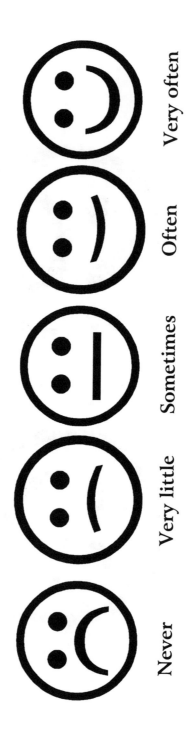

Never   Very little   Sometimes   Often   Very often

I like TV:

| Hate it | Not much | Don't mind | A little | A lot |

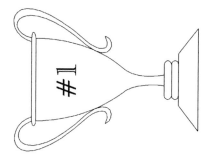

Favorite show?

My favorite person on TV is:

Santa Claus is a real person who brings us presents on Christmas Eve.

True   Not true   Not sure

Superman and Batman are really flying in the movies.

True

Not true

Not sure

If you wish hard when you blow out your birthday candles, your wish will come true.

True

Not true

Not sure

If people on TV adventure shows have a fight, they don't really hurt each other.

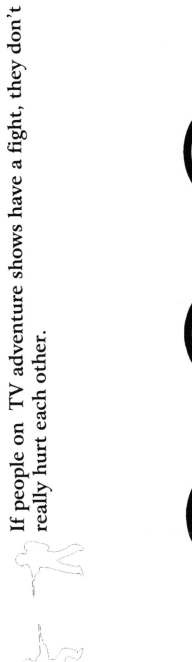

True   Not true   Not sure

There needs to be violence on TV to make the programs exciting.

True   Not true   Not sure

Programs like 'Full House' and 'The Cosby Show' happen in somebody's real house.

True

Not true

Not sure

TV ads make toys and candy look much nicer than they really are.

True

Not true

Not sure

Superman and Batman aren't really flying in the movies; it's a trick.

True   Not true   Not sure

It's allright to make toys and candy look much nicer on TV because then children will want to buy them.

True

Not true

Not sure

In news programs, the people who read the news in the studio are called 'anchors'. Are they by themselves in the studio?

Yes

No

Not sure

OPEN ENDED QUESTION SHEET FOR YOUNGER CHILDREN
(TO BE ADMINISTERED ORALLY IF POSSIBLE)

If you said "no" to the last question, who else is in the studio with the anchors?

Why do you think the people who tell us the news are called "anchors"?

Why is the Count in Sesame Street called the Count?

How do the pictures change on TV? Write the answer in your own words or you can draw your own pictures of how it's done. (Use the other side of the page if you need to.)

Who makes TV programs?

How do they get the money to make the programs?

A book I read this week was:

Say what this book was like in your own words.

Appendix B

Questionnaire for Third, Fourth, and Fifth Graders

UNDERSTANDING TV QUESTIONNAIRE

DR. MÁIRE DAVIES, ANNENBERG SCHOOL FOR COM-MUNICATIONS

Thank you for agreeing to help me find out what children think of television. There are some questions below that I'd like you to answer.

For some questions, you have different choices: I want you to put a circle around the answer that you choose.

For some questions, you can write the answer in your own words. You can write as much or as little as you like. If you don't know the answer, it doesn't matter: just write Don't Know.

If you don't understand the question, please put up your hand and we'll try to help you. Please don't ask another child. We want to know what YOU think. You can be completely honest. We won't use your name when we talk or write about your answers.

Thanks again.

INFORMATION ABOUT YOU

1. Name
2. Age   Date of birth
3. Country you were born in
4. Second language
5. School   Grade

Now for some questions about you and TV: Please put a circle around the answer that applies to you.

YOU AND TV

6. Do you have a video recorder at home?   YES   NO
7. Do you have a video camera at home?   YES   NO
8. Have you ever programmed a VCR?   YES   NO
9. Have you ever used a video camera?   YES   NO
10. Does anyone in your house work with television or radio or film?
                                                   YES   NO

Now for some questions about watching TV: Please put a circle around the number that applies to you. For example, if you watch TV very little, put a circle around the number 2.

11. I watch TV:

1.	2.	3.	4.	5.
Never	Very little	Sometimes	Often	Very Often

12. I like TV:

1.	2.	3.	4.	5.
A lot	A little	Don't mind	Not much	Hate it

13. My favorite TV show is:

14. I like this show because:

15. My favorite person on TV is:

16. I like this person because:

WHAT ARE YOUR VIEWS?

Now here are some questions about the different things that people believe in, including the things they see on TV. Circle the number that applies to you. For example, if you believe that Santa is real, circle number 1. If you don't think he's real, circle 2. If you're not sure, circle 3.

17. Santa Claus is a real person who brings us presents on Christmas Eve.

1.	2.	3.
True	Not true	Not sure

18. Superman and Batman are really flying in the movies.

1.	2.	3.
True	Not true	Not sure

19. If you wish hard when you blow out your birthday candles, your wish will come true.

1.	2.	3.
True	Not true	Not sure

20. If people on TV adventure shows have a fight, they don't really hurt each other.

1.	2.	3.
True	Not true	Not sure

21. There needs to be violence on TV to make the programs exciting.

1.	2.	3.
True	Not true	Not sure

22. Programs like *Full House* and *The Cosby Show* happen in somebody's real house.

1.	2.	3.
True	Not true	Not sure

23. TV ads make toys and candy look much nicer than they really are.

1.	2.	3.
True	Not true	Not sure

24. Superman and Batman aren't really flying in the movies; it's a trick.

1.	2.	3.
True	Not true	Not sure

25. It's alright to make toys and candy look much nicer on TV because then children will want to buy them.

1.	2.	3.
True	Not true	Not sure

26. In news programs, the people who read the news in the studio are called "anchors." Are they by themselves in the studio?

1.	2.	3.
Yes	No	Not sure

27a. If you said "no" to question 26, who else is in the studio with the anchors?

27b. Why do you think the people who tell us the news are called "anchors"?

28. Why is the Count in Sesame Street called the Count?

29. How do the pictures change on TV? Write the answer in your own words or you can draw your own pictures of how it's done. (Use the other side of the page if you need to.)

Appendix C

*Sample Interview Transcript,
First Grade Boy*

Interview with Jack; First grade

April 28, 1993

Int: Why did you press the pause button?

Jack: [*Sesame Street*] Because when you find treasures, they don't usually see Ts on the ground.

Int: Why couldn't that happen?

Jack: Because it could only happen on a board if someone painted it or something. I don't think it would happen on sand.

Int: Now you can press it.

Jack: Now that couldn't happen either. There couldn't be T treasures.

Int: Wouldn't be a treasure chest full of Ts?

Jack: Right.

Int: Why do you suppose they have this treasure chest full of Ts?

Jack: Because they had a big T on the ground and it may be all about Ts.

Int: Why do you think in real life there wouldn't be a chest full of Ts?

Jack: Because there is no such thing as a golden T, but maybe pirates had the little coins that were gold. They didn't have any golden Ts.

Int: Right.

Jack: The blocks can't move themselves.

Int: How do you think they get them to move like that?

Jack:	Maybe they have a little invisible string and they can pull it on the ground.
Int:	So you say that there is no bird like that. Why do you say that?
Jack:	Because maybe in the movie they could have that, but there is no such thing as a giant bird. People don't let birds in their house.
Int:	How do you think Big Bird is made?
Jack:	They put strings on the top of his head and someone was holding these little handles. What do you call those puppets?
Int:	Marionettes?
Jack:	They have like a cardboard bird and they paint him yellow and they make his eye and mouth so it can move. They make his feet like kind of like bendy and his wings and neck are bendy, but they don't have his eyes bendy. His eyes just go like that and his mouth goes like that. They make some spots where it is loose except where his belly is.
Jack:	[*Real News*] People don't say "eeny, meeny, miny, moe" when they are talking about the president.
Int:	Okay.
Jack:	People can't fly sideways and they can't go up and swash their heads. People can't swirl their head around and like have two heads.
Int:	How do you think they have done this with these colors?
Jack:	Maybe they have done this with a computer and they put pictures that they made.
Int:	Why do you think that they would do this?
Jack:	Maybe they are going to tell what's going to happen tomorrow.
Int:	What do you mean by that?
Jack:	Maybe it is like the song in the beginning. Some TV shows always have a part when they begin the show and then they sing the song. They did begin the show and then sing the song and maybe starting the beginning of the song.
Int:	Pause that for a second. Do you know what special effects are?
Jack:	Yeah. They are like when they do something special and it's hard to believe that they did it.

Int: Did you notice any other special effects in that thing that you saw?

Jack: They made him walk faster and people can't walk that fast.

Int: When you mentioned the going faster than normal, how come you didn't mentioned it the first time?

Jack: I didn't notice it.

Int: What kind of program was that we just saw?

Jack: It was like a toy program and he wanted money because there were lots of presents he wanted to buy. He got them all because the guy paid him a little bit.

Int: How is the program that we saw different from the first program?

Jack: The first one that we saw had a couple of cartoons and this one didn't have any cartoons.

Int: What was the first program we saw? How would you describe that?

Jack: Well, well . . .

Int: What kind of people would watch the first program?

Jack: Maybe some little kids. I used to watch it, but I don't any more.

Int: Do you think that the first program was a good program?

Jack: Yeah.

Int: How about the second program? Do you think that was a good program?

Jack: Yeah.

Int: Why do you think the first program was a good program?

Jack: Really, I don't know because I didn't see the whole thing.

Int: Okay.

Jack: But it looked good.

Int: Why do you think that it looked good?

Jack: It might have been a good TV show if I had watched enough of it.

Int: Let's keep going.

Jack: People can't disappear.

Int: [*Cosby Show*] Let's talk about the show that we just saw first and then we will talk about this. Did you notice any special effects in the last thing that we saw?

Jack: No.

Int: What kind of program was that we just saw?

Jack: Some people may watch it like big people. I don't know what else.

Int: How is that program different from the ones before that we had just seen?

Jack: The one before, it had some special effects and they were running fast. This one didn't have special effects and they didn't have any running fast.

Int: What kind of people would watch the program that we just saw?

Jack: Maybe teenagers.

Int: Do you think that was a good program that you just saw?

Jack: Yeah.

Int: Why do you think that was a good program?

Jack: Oh wait! There was one special effect in that.

Int: What was that?

Jack: I never knew that a little three-years-old can beat a seventeen-year-old.

Int: So that doesn't happen in real life?

Jack: No.

Int: Why do you suppose they have her beating the older kid in checkers?

Jack: They set up the board like she was beating him and then they left out the space where they wanted him to go. He went there and she double jumped him.

Int: Why do you suppose they set up the board that way?

Jack: So it would look like she was winning.

Int: Who do you think made that last program? Do you have any idea?

Jack: I don't know. Bill Cosby?

Int: [*The Sand Fairy*] Yeah. Alright. Now you said a person doesn't appear like that and suddenly appear. Why do you suppose they have him suddenly appear like that here?

Jack: Maybe magic or a trick. Maybe they made a whole glass box, but it was a mirror and you can see the guy. He got out of the mirror and it looked like he was really there. See how he stepped there?

Int: He looked like he came out of a mirror.

Jack: Yeah. It was a big mirror.

Int: Okay.

Jack: One thing that I forgot. You can't blow into a sword and make that noise.

Int: So you think someone else made that noise later?

Jack: Yeah.

Int: How do you think they did that?

Jack: They had some kind of special instrument and he just put the sword in his mouth and pretended that he blew. When he blew, someone else blew some instrument.

Int: Why do you suppose they did that? Why do you suppose they had someone else blow the horn?

Jack: Because when you blow in the sword, nothing will happen and it won't make noises. It would have to have like a tube and it doesn't have a tube.

Int: Did you see any other special effects there?

Jack: The baby was sitting on air.

Int: Why do you think they had the baby sitting on air like that?

Jack: Maybe they had like a mirror chair and he might had been like on a chair and that is how he probably did it. Maybe some of it was computer.

Int: What kind of a program was this that we just saw?

Jack: It was like the olden days. It was like a castle kind like sometimes in fairy tales they have castles.

Int: What sort of people watch the program that we just saw?

Jack: I don't know.

Int: How is that program different from the one we saw just before that?

Jack: The one before that, they were living in a house and that one, they were living in a castle.

Int: Do you think the last program was a good program?

Jack: Yeah.

Int: Why do you think that it was a good one?

Jack: I thought it was going to be a scary one when they went down there and I started to like it. When I saw the guy jump out of nowhere, I thought it was going to be pretty bad. It was good, but it was a lot of special effects on that one.

Int: What were the other special effects that you remember seeing?

Jack: When he blew into the sword and people can't jump out of nowhere. I don't know.

Int: I think that will close it up.

Appendix D

*Sample Interview Transcript,
First Grade Girl*

Interview with Anna, First Grade Girl

May 6, 1993

Int: When you see or hear something that couldn't really happen in real life, press the pause button.

Int: Why did you stop?

Anna: [*Sesame Street*] Because people don't paint Ts on the ground and that isn't a real treasure, that's a T.

Int: Why is there a T on the ground? Why do you think?

Anna: Because they want it to be there.

Int: Press play and let's see what happens.

Int: Why did you press it?

Anna: Because there isn't any echo thing that has Ts on it. It's like a T here, here, and there in places.

Int: So what is wrong with that? Why do it that way?

Anna: Because there already isn't a treasure that has Ts.

Int: So why are they using Ts?

Anna: Because they are using it for like 4 months to 5 years in age and they can learn the alphabet.

Int: Let's carry on.

Anna: Because blocks can't move by themselves.

Int: Why not?

Anna: Because they are not alive.

Int: Right. So how are they doing that?

Anna: Just a picture really, that's on TV.

Int: Okay. Keep going.

Anna: Same thing.

Int: If you see the same thing, you don't have to pause it.

Anna: There is no such thing as Big Bird.

Int: What is Big Bird?

Anna: It is really a person and the neck is part of the costume.

Int: Right. Why do they have Big Bird in this program?

Anna: To help them to learn. There are usually number things and alphabet things and some other things, but I think I'm not going to tell you them all.

Int: You don't have to do that. I'm just interested in Big Bird. Carry on.

Anna: Big Bird can't talk. Only the person can.

Int: Who is talking?

Anna: The person.

Int: The person where?

Anna: In the costume.

Int: Right. Let's keep going.

Int: Okay. Just a couple of questions. What kind of program is that?

Anna: Learning.

Int: What sort of people would watch it?

Anna: I know someone who wouldn't.

Int: Who's that?

Anna: My brother.

Int: How old is he?

Anna: Five.

Int: Why wouldn't he watch it?

Anna: Because all he does is watch cartoons and play with his toys and color.

Int: And he doesn't want to watch *Sesame Street*? You don't know why?

Anna: No.

Int: Do you watch it?

Anna: Not really. I watch some shows that are after *Sesame Street* in the afternoon. I think it's called *Square 1, 2, 3* with a lot of math things.

Int: Do you think *Sesame Street* is a good show?

Anna: For learning. Not for watching cartoons.

Int: Let's see what's coming next. Press play.

Int: Why did you press pause?

Anna: Actually I didn't want to.

Anna: [ads] There is such a toy.

Int: There isn't such a toy?

Anna: No! There is such a toy.

Int: You didn't press it then. Did you notice anything that wasn't like real life?

Anna: [*Real News for Kids*] People don't usually give other people money.

Int: Anything else?

Anna: I do not know anyone who would get that many toys in a toy store. My brother would like to, but no one would let him.

Int: Why do you think they did that? What was that news item telling us? Do you know what it was all about?

Anna: It was a commercial for toys.

Int: And what do commercials do?

Anna: They try to make people want to buy their things.

Int: What about the way the guy was moving? Was he moving in a normal way?

Anna: No. People don't usually run like that in a store.

Int: Why was he doing that? How did they make him look so fast?

Anna: So the commercial wouldn't take an hour.

Int: I see. Should we carry on? Press play and see what's coming next. One more question about that program. What kind of a program was it?

Anna: A commercial.

Int: Okay.

Int: Well you didn't press very much there. Did that seem like real life to you?

Anna: [*Cosby Show*] Not really, but I didn't know what to press.

Int: You didn't see anything that wasn't like real life?

Anna: It sort of was and it sort of wasn't.

Int: What wasn't like real life?

Anna: I think it seemed real, but it really was just a TV show.

Int: I see. What is the difference between real and a TV show?

Anna: A TV show really never happened and it is happening on the stage. When like someone is out, you don't see them behind the curtains.

Int: I see. Who are those people?

Anna: I forget because I don't watch a lot of TV.

Int: You didn't recognize the program?

Anna: I sort of recognize the people.

Int: Do you know the name of the program?

Anna: Uh . . .

Int: What kind of a program is that?

Anna: Uh . . .

Int: It doesn't matter if you don't know.

Anna: Uh . . .

Int: How is it different from the other program that you just saw?

Anna: The other one is more real and that really isn't. It is more like cartoonish one

Int: What is this one?

Anna: Cartoonish.

Int: Is it?

Anna: Uh huh.

Int: What about these people laughing? Who are they? Where did that laughter come from?

Anna: I forget.

Int: You can't guess? The laughing people. Do you know who they were?

Int: Who was laughing? The people?

Anna: The people.

Int: Why do people laugh?

Anna: Because they're embarrassed.

Int: That's a good reason. Do you think that was funny?

Anna: No.

Int: Let's watch the next one.

Anna: What is this?

Int: A program called *The Sand Fairy*.

Int: Why did you stop?

Anna: Because people don't usually hang out windows because they can get killed.

Int: Right.

Anna: There usually aren't stairs that tight.

Int: So where are they? Any idea? Have a guess.

Anna: No.

Int: Let's keep going and we might find out.

Int: Why have you stopped?

Anna: Babies can't float in the air.

Int: How is that baby floating?

Anna: It's probably tied up.

Int: Why do you think it is done that way? What do you think is going on here? Why is that baby floating?

Anna: It is probably a war.

Int: A war.

Anna: People tied the baby up from the other side.

Int: Right. What made you think there was a war going on?

Anna: Because of the knights.

Int: Keep going.

Anna: High chair is not there.

Int: Right. So is she telling the truth? Why does she say he is sitting in his high chair?

Anna: [silence]

Int: Okay, let's keep going.

Anna: It looks like she is holding something, but she really isn't.

Int: You can't see what she is holding? So what is going on?

Anna: Everything is being invisible.

Int: Is it? Why do you think that is?

Anna: The sand fairy.

Int: Right. Let's keep going.

Int: Well that's the end. What sort of a program was that?

Anna: Fairy tale sort of.

Int: Have you seen that program? Have you read the book about the sand fairy?

Anna: I don't see it on TV.

Int: No. Well that is a book called *Five Children and It* and maybe you might read that book one day. It is a story based on a book. Do you think that was any good? Do you think it was interesting?

Anna: Not really.

Int: How is it different from the other things we have seen?

Anna: There were knights and there were only children at the beginning.

Int: Where do you think those children live?

Anna: And it was only black and white.

Int: Right.

Int: And where do you think those children live? Were they American children?

Anna: No.

Int: How do you know they are not American children? What makes you say that?

Anna: [silence]

Int: Okay. We are finished.

Appendix E

Sample Interview Transcript, Third Grade Boy

Interview with Elijah, Third Grade Boy

April 28, 1993

Int: These are a little bit different pieces of programs that we are going to see. First we'll see *Sesame Street*. Ready? Anything that couldn't happen in real life.

Int: Okay. What was happening there?

Elijah: The blocks were moving by themselves.

Int: And why couldn't that happen in real life?

Elijah: Because it is impossible for blocks to move by themselves.

Int: So how do you think they're doing it?

Elijah: By strings.

Int: Right.

Elijah: Fishing strings. They're clearer.

Int: And what's the point of doing it that way?

Elijah: I don't know.

Int: Okay. Let's keep going.

Elijah: He couldn't be real because he is too big of a bird. Birds can be that big when they were dinosaurs.

Int: Right. So what is Big Bird then?

Elijah: He is a mask, a costume.

Int: So why do they do it that way?

Elijah: So it's more fun to watch.

Int: Okay. Keep going.

Int: Okay. That is the end of *Sesame Street*. What sort of a program is it?

Elijah: A children's program like from 3 to 5.

Int: How do you know that?

Elijah: Because that the ages that are watching it.

Int: You don't watch it anymore?

Elijah: No.

Int: What do you think of the program?

Elijah: It's okay for little kids. But not for older kids.

Int: Right. Now we are going to see a program called *Real News for Kids* and there are some ads first. So again, if there is anything that couldn't happen in real life, press pause. You want to press play?

Elijah: He didn't run that fast.

Int: So what's happening there?

Elijah: They're doing something with the camera. They're doing something special with the picture.

Int: Why do you think that they're doing it like that?

Elijah: So it looks better and it seems faster.

Int: And when you say they're doing it, who are the people that are doing it?

Elijah: The cast.

Int: Right.

Int: Okay. So there were a lot of special effects there.

Elijah: Yeah.

Int: But you didn't press the pause. Why not?

Elijah: I pressed it once. But there was another thing that couldn't happen. They couldn't go from all those people that fast.

Int: Which people?

Elijah: The people who were saying Ross Perot, Ross Perot.

Int: Right. So how did they do that?

Elijah: Special effects.

Int: Why do they do it that way rather than just do it slowly?

Elijah: Because it wastes some time and they need time for commercials.

Int: Do you think it helps people to understand what's happening?

Elijah: Not really, because most of the important part stays slower.

Int: So that people can understand?

Elijah: Yeah.

Int: Did you understand?

Elijah: Yeah.

Int: Good. Now what kind of a show was that?

Elijah: A news show that most kids can understand so they put it in their language.

Int: What sort of people would watch it?

Elijah: Kids.

Int: Right. Do you think that it was any good?

Elijah: It was okay.

Int: Just okay?

Elijah: It was good.

Int: What's really good in your opinion?

Elijah: On that show?

Int: Yeah. Could you think of anything that was really good?

Elijah: I liked it all.

Int: Do you watch it?

Elijah: Sometimes.

Int: Let's watch the next one. Do you want to press play? Let's watch *The Cosby Show*. Do you watch *The Cosby Show*?

Elijah: Yeah.

Elijah: All those people in the background couldn't really be there laughing. It has to be on stage or they put the laughing in it.

Int: What has to be on stage?

Elijah: The show.

Int: They put the laughing in it?

Elijah: Yeah.

Int: How do they do that?

Elijah: They record it and they push play.

Int: Okay. You didn't press much there?

Elijah: No.

Int: Why was that?

Elijah: Because it is an adult show and it can't have much things that can't happen.

Int: Right. What kind of a program is it?

Elijah: It is a comedy.

Int: And what sort of audience or what sort of people?

Elijah: People who like comedy.

Int: Do you like comedy?

Elijah: Yes.

Int: What do you think of that program?

Elijah: It's okay.

Int: Just okay?

Elijah: Good.

Int: You are not going to hand out a lot of praise freely. Why is it good?

Elijah: Because it is funny.

Int: And funny is good?

Elijah: Yeah.

Int: Last one coming up. This is called *The Sand Fairy* and you'll see what happens.

Elijah: He couldn't come out of thin air.

Int: Right. So how do you think that they do it?

Elijah: I think I saw this movie and he came out of the closet.

Int: Right. Okay.

Elijah: That can't happen.

Int: Why not?

Elijah: Because it is impossible for a baby to be up in thin air.

Int: So what do you think's happening here?

Elijah: They're either holding him or he is sitting on a chair with a picture on the front.

Int: Right. Keep going.

Elijah: She didn't stir anything because she didn't have a spoon.

Int: What's she doing? What's happening here?

Elijah: They are all witches or something.

Int: What makes you say that?

Elijah: Because they're doing magic.

Int: Right. Okay.

Int: What do you think is happening there?

Elijah: The kids got there somehow and something is happening to the village and they want to know what is happening. Because they're bringing all these soldiers to stop somebody.

Int: And where did that take place?

Elijah: In like Italy.

Int: Where do you think the program was made?

Elijah: In Universal Studios.

Int: Right. What about the clothes they were wearing?

Elijah: They paid people to probably make them or they already had old clothes.

Int: So when was this happening? When was the program meant to be happening?

Elijah: Like early 1800s.

Int: What gave you that idea?

Elijah: Because the background and stuff and the clothes that they wearing.

Int: What kind of program is that?

Elijah: Fiction program.

Int: Right. Fiction program. What sort of people might watch it?

Elijah: Young kids.

Int: What did you think of it?

Elijah: It was okay.

Appendix F

Sample Interview Transcript, Fourth Grade Girl

Interview with Lauren,
Fourth Grade Girl

May 6, 1993

Int: As soon as you see something that isn't in real life, press pause.

Lauren: There really couldn't be a big T on the ground.

Int: Why not?

Lauren: Because it is in a deserted island.

Int: Where does it come from? Why do you think it is like that?

Lauren: Because a lot of times X marks the spot and they're teaching kids a different letter.

Int: Yeah. So they use the T instead of the X?

Lauren: Yeah.

Int: Let's keep going.

Lauren: If it was a treasure it wouldn't be all Ts like that.

Int: Why not?

Lauren: Why would someone bury a treasure with all these all Ts?

Int: If they were gold they might. So what's the point of that? Why do something that is not real?

Lauren: To teach you about the letter T.

Int: Why don't they just say that this is the letter T?

Lauren: Because people don't really care. Little kids watch it.

Int: Little kids watch it?

Lauren: Blocks don't really move around.

Int: How is it being done?

Lauren: First they stop the film and they move it and they stop it and they fix it and they start the film again.

Int: Have you done something like this?

Lauren: No.

Int: But you know how it is done? How do you know?

Lauren: Because I watched some stuff on special effects.

Lauren: Bird is not talking.

Int: So who is talking here?

Lauren: Him. Big Bird can't talk.

Lauren: If he was really playing the piano, the phone would ring but the piano doesn't make that sound. You could see that he touched the keys when the phone rang.

Int: So what is the point?

Lauren: I don't know yet.

Int: Then we will see.

Lauren: Every time he did it again, the door would ring. They're just trying to make it so that every time he does it that something happens.

Int: Any idea why?

Lauren: No.

Int: What's the effect of that?

Lauren: Teach people the different sounds.

Int: Anything else?

Lauren: No.

Int: What would you think if that kept happening to you?

Lauren: Maybe there was something going on that I didn't know about.

Int: Right.

Int: What sort of program is that?

Lauren: Educational.

Int: Educational program. How would you know?

Lauren: They teach little kids fun things and how to read and write.

Int: And who would watch it?

Lauren: Little kids like from 2 to about 4 or 5.

Int: But not you?

Lauren: No.

Int: Why not?

Lauren: Because we already know this stuff.

Int: Do you like the program?

Lauren: Yeah.

Int: Okay. Next clip coming up. This is a news program, but there are some ads first.

Lauren: They have the clippings of a kid upside down.

Int: The kid upside down?

Lauren: I know it is just a clipping, but . . .

Int: What do you mean by clipping?

Lauren: A clipping is where they take pictures and they put them onto backgrounds to make it look like it is on tape.

Int: I see. Why do you think that they do it this way?

Lauren: Because it looks like they use computer graphic to tell what is computer and what is not.

Int: And what's the point of doing it that way?

Lauren: It makes them know what's on. It makes it look good.

Int: Do you think it looks good? Do you like it?

Lauren: Yeah.

Lauren: Because they had different people from all over and that couldn't really be that in one TV studio. You would have to film it from all different places.

Int: So you are referring to the bit where they had one person and then another person.

Lauren: People are all over the country and they have to use special equipment to get them all together.

Int: What is the point of doing that?

Lauren: To tell you all the different views and what everyone is talking about. You don't have to wait with just one and you can get people from all over the world and tape them and bring them back to where you're shooting the actual video.

Int: Does that make it easy?

Lauren: It makes it easy on the news people to be able to go and actually talk to people like satellite over in another part of the world.

Lauren: Couldn't really go that fast. They are speeding up the film and they're making the clip go faster.

Int: Any reason do you think?

Lauren: Because they have to fit it all into one time slot.

Int: Why are they speeding it up?

Lauren: It makes people want to watch it because it just does. It gets in people's minds in the way they use graphics. It makes people say that they like the graphics in that show and the special effects.

Lauren: No store manager would give someone money.

Int: Why do you think they are doing it?

Lauren: To finance the show and get money.

Int: Do you think that they're trying to teach you anything?

Lauren: To teach kids that if you ask for money that you might get it.

Int: What was the point in that? Do you know what that news item was about?

Lauren: It was about how a lot of people don't have that much money anymore and how you can't always get all you want and how some people are strong and stuff. How the economy is not very good.

Int: How is that different from *Sesame Street*?

Lauren: This is for older kids to show them what's going on in the world.

Int: And *Sesame Street*?

Lauren: For young kids to read and write.

Int: Next program coming up.

Lauren: [*Cosby Show*] In real life you wouldn't have people clapping behind you and every time that you do something funny, everyone would clap.

Int: So what is the point of having that?

Lauren: It make people laugh and enjoy the show because it tells them when to laugh. It gives them a sense that other people like the show.

Int: Do you think it is funny? Do you agree?

Lauren: Yeah.

Int: You didn't press much there. Why not?

Lauren: Because it is sitcom and it is supposed to be real life.

Int: And do you think it is like real life?

Lauren: Uh huh, sort of.

Int: How is it like real life?

Lauren: Sometimes in shows they put the same situations that some families have and different stuff like about school. And that's for like entertainment.

Int: And it is like real life too?

Lauren: Yeah.

Int: So how is sitcom different from news?

Lauren: News is more about what is going on in the world and it's more informative.

Lauren: [*Sand Fairy*] Stop there. No one can appear like that.

Int: So what do you think is happening?

Lauren: Probably a fiction thing about magic.

Int: And how is it done?

Lauren: First they clip it without him and they stop it and then they put him in and they start it again.

Int: What do you mean they?

Lauren: The people on the camera.

Lauren: I don't get it, but they are talking about wishing for something and that it came true.

Int: And you think . . .

Lauren: That he is granting their wish.

Int: So why are we stopping?

Lauren: Because no one really grants wishes.

Int: That is a shame.

Lauren: No kids would shoot bows and arrows.

Lauren: Are you talking about now because it is back in the medieval times and it is couldn't happen now.

Int: What couldn't really happen?

Lauren: This couldn't really happen now, but it could happen in earlier times. Well, not the magic part but having the knights and stuff.

Int: So what are you saying?

Lauren: It's the past.

Int: And when was the program made?

Lauren: Program?

Int: Yeah. When was it made? When was this show made?

Lauren: When was it supposed to be taking place?

Int: Tell me when it was supposedly taking place.

Lauren: In the medieval times.

Int: And how do you know that?

Lauren: Because of the knights and armor and the way the horses were clothed and stuff like that.

Int: What about the children?

Lauren: And the clothes that they were wearing.

Int: Are they medieval clothes?

Lauren: Yeah.

Int: But it is taking place in medieval times?

Lauren: Yeah.

Int: When was the program made? Was it made in medieval times?

Lauren: No. Present.

Int: How do you know that?

Lauren: They taped it. You don't know?

Int: That's what I am trying to get at. You're not saying that it was made then?

Lauren: Yeah.

Int: Okay. So who are these people?

Lauren: They're actors.

Lauren: Stop! You really don't have music playing in real life. You don't really have music playing when you are walking down the steps.

Int: So where is that coming from?

Lauren: From speakers to make the effects more realistic.

Int: And what is the effect?

Lauren: Different kinds of music. Some music makes it suspenseful and it tells you when something exciting is going to happen.

Int: And what is this music?

Lauren: This music is like hurrying and trying to get where they are going and they are trying to find things. It also helps you to get a feel of what's going on.

Int: Are you a musical person?

Lauren: No. I don't play music.

Int: How do you know this stuff?

Lauren: I don't know. I watch one show and it's called *Young Riders* and they use a lot of music in that show.

Int: Right.

Lauren: No one really floats like that.

Int: How is that done?

Lauren:

They have attached clear ropes that you can't see or ropes that certain colors can't be seen by film.

Int: So it is a rope?

Lauren: Probably a rope.

Lauren: If it was a high chair you would be able to see it.

Int: Okay.

Lauren: But there is obviously something going on because he is just floating in thin air and she doesn't notice it.

Int: Uh huh. Who doesn't notice it?

Lauren: The maid.

Int: How do you know that she is a maid?

Lauren: Because of the clothes that she was wearing and what she was doing.

Int: Right. Which was?

Lauren: She was doing the cooking and stuff like that.

Int: What do you think is going on?

Lauren: I have no idea.

Int: So what kind of a program is that?

Lauren: That was a fiction.

Int: And what sort of people would it be for?

Lauren: Children.

Int: What age?

Lauren: My age or about seven to twelve.

Int: Would you watch it?

Lauren: I don't know if I would, but my brother and sisters probably would for entertainment.

Int: What about the way the children spoke?

Lauren: They were English.

Int: How do you know?

Lauren: The way they spoke.

Appendix G

Sample Interview Transcript, Fifth Grade Boy

Interview with Ben, Fifth Grade Boy

April 28, 1993

Int: As soon as you see or hear anything that could not happen in reality and in real life, you press pause.

Ben: He couldn't dig that fast.

Int: Okay, so how are they doing it?

Ben: It's just a cartoon and all cartoons are like that. And another thing: if he was really looking for a treasure, it wouldn't be just one man. There'd be a whole crew.

Int: Okay, when you say, "just a cartoon" . . .

Ben: Well, cartoons are not real and anyway, it's just one thing if you're watching like a sitcom reality, but that's just they make it look like it's real. But cartoons, you know it's not supposed to be real.

Int: How is it different?

Ben: It's different because it just wouldn't happen. It'd be a whole crew and he couldn't dig that fast. Nobody could dig that fast, not even Superman.

Int: So why is it done that fast?

Ben: So you won't have to wait forever. Like, in reality, it'd be like (makes sound).

Int: Okay, keep going.

Ben: Blocks can't move themselves. They're moving it with fishing line, I would guess. Or they would, what they would do is, they would do just like I'm doing, like, take the block like that. Okay? Shoot one—24 frames in a second—then stop it, move, stop, move, stop, move.

Int: So, again, what's the point of doing this?

Ben: It's just like a . . . there's no real point. It's just like clever and they do it, stuff like that.

Int: Okay, go on.

Ben: [stops tape] Well, I think there might be some certain smell to that or something because cats aren't attracted. That doesn't even really look like a cat.

Int: So what's not real?

Ben: Well, a cat wouldn't be attracted to blocks like that. I don't think it even really looks like a cat that much.

Int: Do you think it is a cat?

Ben: I don't know. That could be a real cat. In fact, I think that is a real cat, because of the motion like that. [stops tape] Right there. Big Bird isn't real.

Int: Big Bird isn't real? You're sure?

Ben: Yeah, I know how they do that.

Int: How?

Ben: Well, let's see. You would have two men to control a puppet like that. Okay. There's a man in here that controls the body movements from the neck down. The head is a robot. Okay, the head is a robot. You look up, you see like that, okay? It's kind of like a mechanical periscope. Like look at it and it goes out little holes in his eyes and to control the mouth movements, there's a guy behind the cameraman. He uses a little joystick. It takes a lot of work to get it just right. He uses that and there's a microphone that he has. So it's kind of like a ventriloquist. You have to talk into the microphone and do the mouth movements in really good time at the same time.

Int: Okay, so Big Bird's not at all real in any way, so what's the point of him?

Ben: Well, just for kids, that they might believe that he's real. A big bird. He teaches kids about triangles and like lessons, you know.

Int: Why a bird rather than a person?

Ben: Well, kids can adapt to that better. Like, um, they listen to people all the time and it's just nicer if it's just like animals like that doing it.

Int: Thank you. Keep going.

Ben: That's not real talking on the phone. That reh-reh-reh.

Int: What is it then?

Ben: It's just nonsense. Reh-reh-reh.

Int: And what's the point of doing it that way?

Ben: Because to little kids, it kind of sounds like that. If you ever listen to someone talk on the phone, you hear like "reh-reh-reh," you know? Except it doesn't sound like (high-pitched) "reh-reh-reh." That kind of sounds like a tape rewinding or something.

Ben: [stops tape] There wouldn't be that much of a coincidence, I don't think. Like when you're about to like, your hands are an inch from the keyboard, and the phone rings, then after that the doorbell rings.

Int: So what's the point of that?

Ben: It's supposed to be kind of funny. Distractions, like, there wouldn't be a point to the story if he taught him the piano by hearing like that. Should I keep going?

Int: What kind of a program is that?

Ben: That is a program for children, preschoolers, toddlers, 2 through 6, who are learning the basics: letters, numbers, shapes, like all that, how to be friends, sex, um, caring.

Int: So who's it aimed at?

Ben: It's aimed at preschoolers, toddlers, 2 through 6.

Int: Did you watch it?

Ben: Yeah, I used to watch it. And, my sister used to watch it when it first started because she's older now; she's 22. And well, it's just for kids like that, for preschoolers.

Int: Do you think it's a good program?

Ben: Yeah, I'd say it's a good program.

Int: Why is it good?

Ben: For, like it's good for kids who are working on learning their numbers because it teaches them in a fun way. Like my little brother, he still looks forward to it every day.

Int: Right. The next one is *Real News for Kids*.

Ben: Okay.

Ben: I wouldn't believe that would come with all that paper. There must be like five or six sets combined.

Int: But why did they do it?

Ben: With all those pens.

Int: Why are they doing it?

Ben: They're doing that so people will think that it will cost a lot, but it really doesn't.

Int: What's the point of people thinking that?

Ben: People really want to buy over priced things for what it really is.

Int: Okay.

Ben: Yeah.

Int: What do you think about that?

Ben: It probably cost a dollar to make them and they probably sell it for thirty.

Int: What do you think about that?

Ben: I would not buy it.

Int: Okay.

Ben: Those sets in the background don't come with it. Actually the kids don't make it. The adults on the crew and maintenance make it. It looks like the kids made it. Actually it doesn't even look like the kids made it. It looks like it comes with the set of dolls itself, but really doesn't.

Int: Again, what is the point of creating that?

Ben: So it looks more exciting than what it really is. The arms probably don't even move.

Int: So what's going on here?

Ben:	They're just trying to get you to buy them. It's like yesterday I was on the bus and these kids they buy these little toys. Little crummy toys they're like about six bucks, action figures and don't even do anything. I mean like it's one thing if you buy something that's worth your money. Like something to invest in like sports cars, stocks, etc. or something like that. Should I keep going?
Int:	Yeah. Keep going.
Ben:	The lady that they just showed I think was on the air for two weeks. And they make toys of it and it's not hot any more.
Ben:	Computer animation. It's not real.
Int:	Okay. What's the point of it?
Ben:	To make it look cool. In fact, it does look cool because if it's not real, people might think that's real and think they might get a real education.
Int:	Who might think it was real?
Ben:	Little kids. Maybe like bums who walks into TV stores in New York City. Just anybody might think that it was real and it isn't. It is just a computer. These computers make images on the computer and they can make it uh, like uh, PS2. They mostly use IBM.
Int:	How would people know that? How did you know that?
Ben:	Because that isn't real. There is nothing that you can see and . . .
Int:	How did you learn about the computer animation?
Ben:	I know. I read it in books. A real lot of this stuff is in books. And like I do it.
Int:	Okay. You do it yourself?
Ben:	Uh, not in computer animation. Like I am not experienced yet in editing, but like I know a little bit about it.
Int:	Great! Well carry on.
Ben:	Some of this is considered animation. This is real and the background is behind the lines.
Ben:	It is real.
Int:	Why do you say that?

Ben: The Vietnam memorial is real. I have seen it before.

Int: Okay.

Ben: Is this uh, during when he [Ross Perot] jumped out and before he jumped back in?

Int: Yes, yes. It was during the campaign.

Ben: Kids would like that and could spend all the time in the toy store and get clothes and other famous hot spots, movies.

Int: So why is he doing it this way?

Ben: Because this is real and these are kids. Like this one I will guess maybe seven to fourteen. He looks seventeen.

Int: Right.

Ben: His friends won't like it. Like all these toys that he is buying them. His friends won't like it. Like all these twelve-year old guys. I sure wouldn't want two thousand dollars just to buy toys.

Int: So what is the point? Why are they doing it this way?

Ben: They're doing it for the story to explain how the government is spending like a kid in the toy store. The guy is lending money for a homeless kid down the street, but it happens that he bought a twenty-five cents monkey that wouldn't work tomorrow. So to this little kid looks like he lend him enough money to buy him a house.

Int: Okay. What kind of program?

Ben: Youth's program.

Int: Audience?

Ben: Audience?

Int: What sort of people?

Ben: Seven to fourteen.

Int: Children?

Ben: Yeah.

Int: Do you think that it is a good program?

Ben: I don't know. I don't know. Some of it isn't real and some of it is probably real. Uh, I don't know. It doesn't really set an example for kids to get a lot of money to go out and waste it all on a toy store. Even if you are buying it from someone else.

Int: Okay.

Ben: I don't know about it. I don't think that I would watch it.

Int: What about all those special effects? You know the camera kept moving and the sound track had music on it. Why didn't you press pause when all that happened?

Ben: You mean like fast forward in the music?

Int: Yeah.

Ben: I don't know how to do all that. I did that with the editing and also with the process audiencer I think. I should have pressed pause then.

Int: It is interesting that you didn't.

Ben: I didn't because I wasn't really thinking.

Int: That's alright. Not to worry. Let us get on with the next little bit. *The Cosby Show.*

Ben: Right.

Ben: That's not real. Dad is a doctor and mom is a lawyer and the house is always clean. A doctor and a lawyer are not going to be in the house all the time playing with teddy bears like that. They are always going to be out doing work and stuff.

Int: What's the point of doing it this way?

Ben: Just so that that can fit in better. Because my dad is a doctor and sometimes he doesn't come home until eleven.

Int: And is your house like this?

Ben: Not as big and my mom is not a lawyer.

Ben: He wouldn't like be at a toy store if he is a doctor even if you did not see the show. He is always there at the house.

Int: Okay. So it would not be likely that doctors and lawyers would have such wonderful lives?

Ben: And, and also what wouldn't be real about it is that no wife would maybe remind the dad or even the kids about the lie he said about how, uh, about that.

Int: What about stuff like the laughter. Where is that coming from?

Ben: That is the laugh track.

Int: Is it?

Ben: Yeah.

Int: What does that mean?

Ben: They have people laughing as if it were a live show. Which it isn't. They have a studio audience and they have cards and when that flashes, it signals the crowd to start clapping. In *The Cosby Show* if it isn't live, there is a lot of people laughing whenever there is a clap and they signal the sound manager to put the laughter on.

Int: Why do they do that?

Ben: Just a way they do it to trick people and to believe that they are doing it live even though they aren't. Just like that.

Int: What sort of a program is it?

Ben: Sitcom. Situation comedy.

Int: What sort of audience? What sort of people is it meant for?

Ben: It is meant for mostly from about 8 to adults.

Int: A big range of ages.

Ben: Yeah.

Int: Do you think it is good? *The Cosby Show*?

Ben: Yeah.

Ben: [*The Sand Fairy*] They're not really looking at that.

Int: They're not really looking at that?

Ben: It's fake. They're not really looking at that.

Int: They're not really looking at that?

Ben: And anyway people won't look out of a window like that. Especially then because you can easily fall down.

Ben: It is all a different set. They're not doing this in the big castle like that.

Int: Then what is the point? What are they trying to do?

Ben: They're just trying to express to you that this film is supposed to be set in a castle, but you know that it really isn't.

Ben: In a dungeon like that, no one would pick up a horn like that and blow it. There is no spider webs in the horn.

Int: So what do you think's going on here?

Ben: They're exploring the castle. It's like they have never been there before.

Int: What does that mean?

Ben: That's fake. They say a baby's just floating there.

Int: And how is it done?

Ben: A technique called green screen. They put everything else in green and they put the baby there. And they place the green in that film with the background so it looks like it is floating and it really isn't.

Ben: He is supposed to be invisible.

Int: What is supposed to be invisible?

Ben: Sitting in the high chair and what they're stewing.

Int: Okay that's it. Do you have any idea what was going on there in that program?

Ben: Yeah.

Int: Do you know the story?

Ben: No. I never seen it.

Int: Have you ever read any of E. Nesbit's books?

Ben: Who?

Int: E. Nesbit.

Ben: No.

Int: Okay. Any idea what was going on in that film?

Ben: I would say that they were going in the castle in hopes that they would find something. And it looked like that lady at the end was her mother because she was asking her to take the child.

Int: And what kind of program would you say that was?

Ben: Drama or adventure.

Int: And what sort of people would be watching?

Ben: Probably twelve through maybe eighteen. Well how big are her books? Would you say like that thick?

Int: Yeah.

Ben: Twelve to maybe twenty. I don't know.

Int: But what do you think of it just from that clip you saw.

Ben: I don't know whether or not I want to watch it. I will watch it a few times and if I like it, fine I'll keep watching it.

Int: Was it an American show?

Ben: No. It was probably produced by the BBC.

Int: What made you think so?

Ben: Because of the English accent.

Int: Okay. That's it. Thank you very much.

Appendix H

Interview Schedule

INTRODUCTION

I'm going to show you some scenes from different TV programs on the video. I want you to hold the remote control and when something happens in the programs that couldn't really happen in real life, I want you to press the pause button. [Start the audio tape at this point.]

[Check that the child understands the instructions and knows how to press pause.]

[When the child presses pause ask:]

  1. Why have you pressed the pause button?
  2. Why couldn't that happen in real life?
  3. Why is it done that way?
  4. If the child uses "they," ask who "they" are.

[Use follow-up questions if the child's answer isn't clear; for instance:] What do you mean by that? or What part of the program are you talking about?

[Otherwise, let the child talk as freely and with as little prompting as possible.]

WHEN EACH CLIP IS OVER

[If the child hasn't commented on special effects ask:]

  1. Did you notice any special effects that the people who made the program used?
  2. [If yes] Why didn't you mention them?
  3. What kind of program was that?
  4. [After first clip:] How was that program different from the one before?
  5. What sort of people would watch that program?
  6. Do you think it's a good program? Why? Why not?

Author Index

231

Subject Index

A

Acting, quality and reality perception on television, 31
Advertising, *see also* Commercials
  falsity and media literacy study, 53
  strategies and tribalism of children, 10
Aesthetics
  awareness and Sand Fairy, 122
  function
    comments from children's question-
      naires, 128–129
    modality judgment, 125–126
African Americans, portrayal on Cosby
    Show, 102, *see also* Cosby Show
Age, *see also* Media literacy, study/sample
  differences
    accounting for illusions in Sand
      Fairy, 115–117
    children's theories of mind, 12
    developmental variation, 9–10
    reality perception on television, 33,
      53, 55
    schemas of interpretation, 42
    significance of misperception, 26
  range for children in media literacy
    study, 50
Agencies, curricular theme in media educa-
    tion, 44
Alienation devices, reality perception on
    television, 30, 32
Altruism, Real News for Kids, 98
Analogy, use on Real News for Kids,
    99–100
Animation

computer and comments from chil-
    dren's questionnaires, 137
Real News for Kids vs. Sesame Street,
    96, 222
stop-frame and reality perception on
    television, 83–84, 87–88, 92
Art
  comments from children's question-
      naires, 127–130
  expression of life, 149–150
  main/subcategories and modality,
    125–126
  postmodern and tele-literacy, 70
  rules of
    Real News for Kids, 96
    reality perception on television,
      33–34
Artistic features/techniques
  cues in Sand Fairy, 122
  distance recognition, 2
Attention span, material selection for
    media literacy study, 78
Attention-getting
  special effects, 35–36
  Real News for Kids, 96–97
Attributions, pragmatic and children,
    18–19, *see also* Pragmatics
Audiences/producers, curricular theme in
    media education, 44–45
Audiovisual media, formal features, 36
Availability, subjects in media literacy
    study, 50
Awareness, television illusions and media
    literacy study, 53, 55–56, *see also*
    Pragmatic awareness

235